99 SIGNS

YOU ARE NOT IN THE 1%

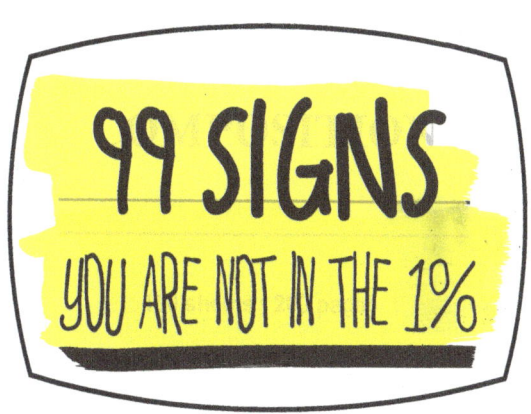

DRAGON FRUIT

Copyright © 2015 by **Mango Media Inc.**

Front Cover Image: S.m. Torres
Back Cover Image: S.m. Torres
Cover Design: Elina Diaz
Interior Design, Theme and Layout: Elina Diaz & S.m. Torres

All rights reserved. No part of this publication may be reproduced, distributed or transmitted in any form or by any means without prior written permission.

S.m. Torres /Mango Media, Inc.
2525 Ponce de Leon, Suite 300
Coral Gables, FL 33134
www.mangomedia.us

99 Signs You Are Not in The 1% / S.m. Torres -- 1st ed.
ISBN 978-1-63353-015-7

"I'VE GOT ALL THE MONEY I'LL EVER NEED, IF I DIE BY FOUR O'CLOCK."

—Henry Youngman

SOME WORDS YOU PROBABLY WON'T READ : AN INTRO

WHEN YOU'VE LIVED YOUR ENTIRE LIFE AS A PART OF THE 99%, SOMETIMES IT'S EASY TO GET BLINDED BY THE DISADVANTAGES AND BEGIN TO RESENT EVERYONE ELSE FOR THE SITUATION YOU'RE IN. BUT SOMETIMES IT'S EASIER TO TAKE THOSE SAME SENTIMENTS AND LAUGH AT HOW RIDICULOUS THEY ARE.

I'VE SPENT MY ENTIRE LIFE STRUGGLING, WHETHER THEY WERE FIRST WORLD PROBLEMS OR LEGITIMATE SHITTY ISSUES, BUT AT THE END OF THE DAY, I COULD ALWAYS JUST LAUGH IT OVER—BECAUSE WHY BOTHER LETTING LIFE GET YOU DOWN? STICK IT TO THE MAN AND REALIZE WHAT GREAT

SITCOMS WERE MADE OF: THE ISSUES OF THE 99%. THE EVERYDAY, REAL-WORLD PROBLEMS WE COMPLAIN ABOUT IN GROCERY LINES TO MAKE NEW FRIENDS, OR THE SILLY STORIES WE COMPLAIN ABOUT TO COWORKERS AND FRIENDS JUST TO GET THE LOAD OFF AND SMILE, OR THE THINGS THAT MAKE US, WELL, *Human.*

PART OF THE APPEAL OF THE 99% IS WE ARE GREAT IN NUMBERS AND WE ARE NOT ALONE. SO SAY WHATEVER TO YOUR PROBLEMS AND TAKE A BREATHER TO CHUCKLE.

AS THEY SAY, BUILDS CHARACTER, MY FRIEND.

Table of Contents

1. THE THINGS YOU DO FOR MONEY... — 9
2. FEAR & LOATHING OUTSIDE THE OFFICE — 31
3. HOME IS WHAT THE WALLET CAN AFFORD — 49
4. FOR THE LOVE OF MONEY — 63
5. SETTLING DOWN INTO NOTHING — 77
6. POPPING TAGS & CLIPPING COUPONS — 89
7. EAT, PRAY, STARVE — 105
8. LOSE WEIGHT LIKE YOU LOSE MONEY — 123
9. THE SACRED HOURS OF THE WEEKEND — 137
10. THE BIG DAYS OF YOUR LITTLE LIFE — 153
11. CONCLUSION — 165

THE THINGS YOU DO FOR MONEY...

LET'S START WITH THE OBVIOUS: YOU ARE POOR AS HELL, MY FRIEND.

THE TOP 1% OWN ABOUT 40% OF THE NATION'S WEALTH IN THE UNITED STATES WHILE YOU BARELY HAVE 40 CENTS OF A DOLLAR IN YOUR POCKET. BUT THAT'S CAPITALISM FOR YOU. WHILE THE ONE-PERCENTERS GO OFF BATHING IN THE TEARS OF ORPHANED CHILDREN AND SPRINKLING FLAKES OF GOLD ONTO THEIR ICE CREAM SUNDAES OR WHATEVER IT IS THAT RICH PEOPLE ARE DOING, YOU HAVE TO COME TO TERMS WITH SELLING YOUR SOUL TO PAY YOUR TAXES.

IF YOU'RE WORKING HARD FOR PENNIES, CHANCES ARE THESE SIGNS ARE GONNA HIT A LITTLE TOO CLOSE TO HOME.

THE THINGS YOU DO FOR MONEY...

YOU'VE GOT 99 RAGS, BUT RICHES AIN'T ONE.

THE FACT OF THE MATTER IS YOU AND MONEY ARE NOT ON GOOD TERMS. THERE ARE RAGS-TO-RICHES STORIES AND THEN THERE'S YOU, BUDDY. YOU'VE HAD MORE THAN ENOUGH HEARTBREAK FROM BOGUS LOTTERY TICKETS AND RIGGED SLOT MACHINES TO KEEP YOU JADED WHEN WATCHING FEEL-GOOD FAMILY BLOCKBUSTERS ABOUT PEOPLE HAVING THEIR DREAMS COME TRUE. ARE YOU ACTUALLY GETTING MAD AT A NINE-YEAR-OLD PROTAGONIST FOR HAVING A SUCCESSFUL DOG-THEMED BUSINESS PLAN? REALLY?

BUT MAN, IF YOU DID WIN, WOULDN'T IT BE NICE TO FINALLY LEAVE THAT SHITTY JOB OF YOURS? AND PAY OFF ALL YOUR DEBTS? AND BECOME FREE AT LAST? YOU KNOW, BE A HUMAN BEING OR SOMETHING.

THE THINGS YOU DO FOR MONEY...

THERE IS NO OTHER HELL LIKE WORKING IN RETAIL OR THE FAST FOOD INDUSTRY.

IF YOU'VE EVER HAD TO WORK IN CUSTOMER SERVICE, CHANCES ARE YOU'VE LOST YOUR FAITH IN HUMANITY LONG, LONG AGO.

YOU USED TO LOOK AT LITTLE OLD LADIES FONDLY UNTIL YOU REALIZED THEY ARE SPAWNS OF EVIL, READILY EQUIPPED WITH EXPIRED COUPONS AND DAMAGED RETURNED GOODS, AND WHO WILL THREATEN THE MANAGER WITH LAWSUITS OVER HOT COFFEE. YOU'VE DECIDED NEVER TO HAVE KIDS, BASED ON THE SNOT-NOSED BRATS SCREECHING FOR TOYS AND HAPPY MEALS.

cheese that doesn't Melt.

BUT NONE OF THAT COMPARES TO THAT TIME YOU HAD TO CLEAN THE BATHROOM.

AND WHEN YOU SAW THAT STALL THAT LOOKED LIKE A MURDER CRIME SCENE MEETS SEWAGE ATOMIC BOMBS, YOU THOUGHT, AW HELL NAH. YOU QUIT, YOU QUIT, YOU QUIT.

THE THINGS YOU DO FOR MONEY...

THE STRUGGLE IS REAL WHEN PEOPLE TELL YOU, "JUST GET A JOB."

OKAY, SO MAYBE QUITTING YOUR JOB MIGHT HAVE BEEN A MISTAKE NOW THAT YOU'VE GOT, LIKE, ZERO CASH. ESPECIALLY WITH NO JOB WAITING FOR YOU. WHEN PEOPLE QUIT IN MOVIES, THERE'S ALWAYS SEEMS LIKE THERE'S SOME GREAT OPPORTUNITY RIGHT AROUND THE CORNER—SO WHERE THE HELL IS YOUR BIG BREAK? YOU'VE GOT SKILLS!—MAYBE? YOU'RE KIND OF PRETTY!—TO SOMEONE! SOMETIMES YOU'RE A GOOD PERSON!

WHAT DOES IT TAKE TO GET MONEY IN YOUR WALLET? IT'S A SAD DAY WHEN YOU REALIZE YOU'VE GOT MORE MONEY IN YOUR BACK POCKET THAN YOU HAVE IN YOUR CHECKING ACCOUNT. AND AS YOU SEND IN JOB APPLICATION AFTER JOB APPLICATION, YOU'RE JUST SHORT OF HITTING THE STREETS WITH A CUP IN HAND AND HOPING FOR THE BEST. BECAUSE HONESTLY, WHAT'S DIGNITY ANYWAY?

JUST GET a Job

OH! OKAY!

SURE THING

WHY DIDN'T I THINK OF THAT?

WORK

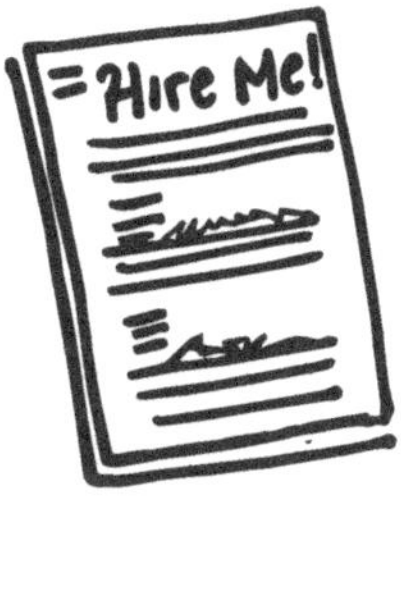
Hire Me!

THINGS I'M GREAT AT

- Organizing shit? Check✓
- Customer Service & shit
- Fluent in Klingon
- Pinning
- Breathing
- Photography (mostly selfies and my Lunch)

THE THINGS YOU DO FOR MONEY...

THAT LOW POINT IN UNEMPLOYMENT WHEN YOU CONTEMPLATE WHICH IS WORSE: BEING HOMELESS OR MOVING BACK IN WITH YOUR PARENTS.

Sometimes life is rough, buddy. Unlike one-percenters who live off trust funds and interest, the rest of the unemployed teeter off the edge of being homeless or moving back home with the ol' ma and pa. Ah, yes, the grand life of continuous eviction notices from both the landlord and your parents. Truly, it is living the dream.

But hey, at least if you move back home, you won't have to pay for rent and food, right? And who knows, maybe your dad knows someone with a job opportunity. Dreams can come true.

BECOME HOMELESS	MOVE BACK IN W/ 'RENTS
• YOU'RE HOMELESS	• ROOF OVER YOUR HEAD
• NO FOOD	• LIKE SO MUCH FOOD. (FREE FOOD)
• YOU CAN GO <u>ANYWHERE</u>	• STILL HAVE A CURFEW.
• WEATHER	• HOT COCOA
• NO BED	• YOUR BED
• FREEDOM?	• PRISON?
• <u>YOU'RE HOMELESS</u>	• <u>UGH</u>. <u>FINE</u>.

THE THINGS YOU DO FOR MONEY...

CONGRATS!

YOU GOT A JOB, AND YOUR BOSS IS... WELL, LET'S JUST SAY YOUR BOSS IS A [GREAT PERSON], A REALLY FREAKING [GREAT PERSON].

LISTEN, WE'VE ALL HAD OUR FAIR SHARE OF TERRIBLE BOSSES. WHETHER IT'S THE PARANOID, JERK-FACED MANAGERS WHO ARE UNDER THE IMPRESSION THAT EVERYONE IS OUT TO STEAL THEIR POSITIONS (BECAUSE, YOU KNOW, THEIR LIFE IS CLEARLY SO MUCH BETTER) OR THE SUPER UNDERQUALIFIED, YOU-DON'T-EVEN-KNOW-HOW-THEY-GOT-THEIR-JOB MANAGERS, SOMEHOW YOU'VE FOUND YOURSELF RANKED BENEATH THEM AND THERE'S NOT MUCH YOU CAN DO ABOUT THAT.

MAYBE ONE DAY YOU CAN "BE YOUR OWN BOSS" LIKE CEOS IN 60 MINUTES INTERVIEWS LIKE TO SAY, BUT FOR NOW, YOU'RE JUST HOPING YOUR BOSS DOESN'T CATCH YOU CHECKING FACEBOOK AND SCROLLING DOWN YOUR TUMBLR DASHBOARD WHILE YOU "WORK."

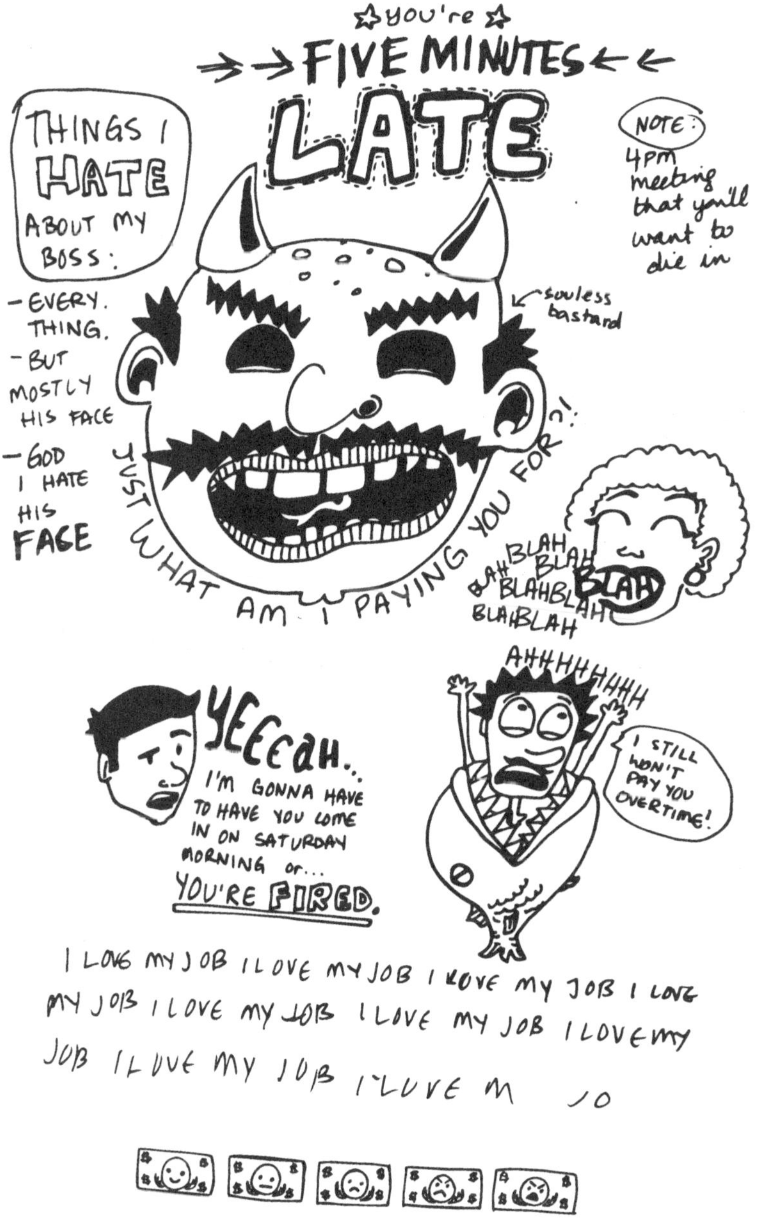

YOU'RE
FIVE MINUTES
LATE
THINGS I HATE ABOUT MY BOSS:
- EVERY. THING.
- BUT MOSTLY HIS FACE
- GOD I HATE HIS FACE
NOTE: 4pm meeting that you'll want to die in
souless bastard
JUST WHAT AM I PAYING YOU FOR?!
BLAH BLAH BLAH BLAH BLAHBLAH BLAH BLAHBLAH BLAH
AHHHHHHHH
YEEEAH... I'M GONNA HAVE TO HAVE YOU COME IN ON SATURDAY MORNING or... YOU'RE FIRED.
I STILL WON'T PAY YOU OVERTIME!
I LOVE MY JOB I LOVE MY JOB I LOVE MY JOB I LOVE MY JOB I LOVE MY JOB I LOVE MY JOB I LOVE MY JOB I LOVE MY JOB I LOVE M JO

THE THINGS YOU DO FOR MONEY...

YOU'LL GET USED TO WORKING IN A CUBICLE, THEY SAID. IT'S <u>NOT</u> THAT BAD, THEY SAID.

SOME GUY IN THE 1960S CAME UP WITH THE CUBICLE SYSTEM AS AN EFFICIENT USE OF SPACE, AND FOR WHAT IT'S WORTH, YOU HATE THAT GUY. WITH THE OFFICE BEING NOTHING BUT A SEA OF GRAY, JUST LIKE THE COLOR OF YOUR DEAD EYES, YOUR CUBICLE HAS THE AESTHETIC APPEAL OF GLUE ON PAPER. THE ONLY DIFFERENCE BETWEEN THIS AND A PRISON CELL IS YOU HAVE A COMPUTER AND A DESK INSTEAD OF A RUSTED TOILET AND A CHAIN BED.

SURE, SOME PEOPLE GET INTO THE SPIRIT AROUND THE HOLIDAYS AND DECORATE THEIR CUBICLE WITH LITTLE DECORATIONS OR

HANG PHOTOS OF LOVED ONES OR TACK STUPID LITTLE CALENDARS OF KITTENS IN TEACUPS ON THE WALL, BUT IT'S ALL A BUNCH OF LIES AND YOU KNOW IT. THE ONLY SAVING GRACE IS THERE IS SOME PRIVACY, SO YOU CAN SQUEEZE IN A QUICK NAP OR DAYDREAM ABOUT LIFE BEYOND THE CUBE. AND YET REALITY STILL COMES CRASHING DOWN ON YOU BECAUSE THE FACT OF THE MATTER IS, YOU'VE GOT...

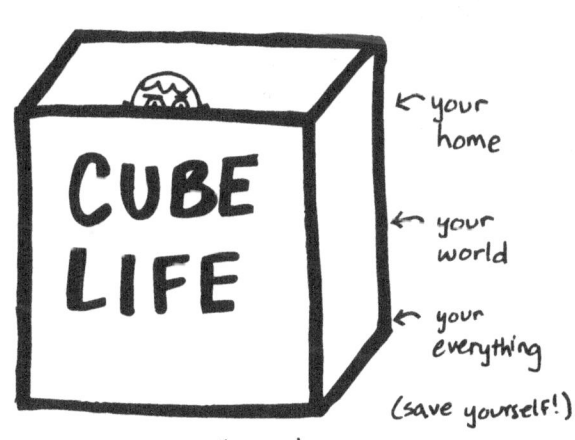

- work with the cube
- love the cube
- be the cube
- never question
- never question the cube

THE THINGS YOU DO FOR MONEY...

...STUDENT LOANS FOREVER AND EVER AND EVER, UNTIL THE DAY YOU DIE, SON.

THERE ARE TIMES WHEN YOU'VE WONDERED... WAS COLLEGE REALLY WORTH IT? LLIKE REALLY, WAS AN $80,000 BACCALAUREATE DEGREE EVEN NECESSARY? BUT IT'S ALRIGHT, MY FRIEND. ALL IN THE NAME OF "HIGHER" EDUCATION. YOUR FANCY LITTLE PAPER DIPLOMA IS A RITE OF PASSAGE NOWADAYS, ALLOWING YOU TO GET A JOB THAT'S NOT EVEN CLOSE TO THE FIELD YOU STUDIED.

EVERY MONTH YOU DIE A LITTLE INSIDE, HAVING TO FORK OVER HALF OF YOUR PAYCHECK TO THE STUDENT LOAN BEAST DEMONS, BUT THE FIGURE NEVER CHANGES WITH THOSE MT. EVEREST-HIGH INTEREST RATES. IF ONLY YOU HAD MORE MONEY...

HEY! YOU GOT A PAY RAISE! HERE'S A DOLLAR. GO WILD, KID.

OKAY, YOU'LL ADMIT IT, WHEN YOU ENVISIONED GETTING YOUR FIRST PAY RAISE, YOU MIGHT HAVE EXPECTED SOMETHING LIKE GETTING PAID THOUSANDS MORE IN YOUR ANNUAL SALARY. PEOPLE MAKE SUCH A BIG DEAL OUT OF IT, YOU JUST ASSUMED. BUT NAH, MAN. YOU'RE LOOKING AT A COUPLE OF CENTS MORE THAN YOUR HOURLY RATE—A DOLLAR, IF YOU'RE LUCKY.

TECHNICALLY, IT'S A PAY RAISE, BUT AS YOU WATCH THE GAS PRICES GO UP THE SAME AMOUNT AS YOUR PAY RAISE, YOU CALL CONSPIRACY ON THIS BULL. IT'S THE SYSTEM TRYING TO BEAT YOU DOWN AGAIN, MAN.

MAKING IT RAIN PENNIES, YO~
gonna invest in some stocks

THE POWER JUST WENT OFF? WHAT A SURPRISE. BUT WHATEVER. NO BIG DEAL. NOT LIKE YOU NEEDED IT OR ANYTHING.

OH, LOOK AT THAT. YOU HAVE NO ELECTRICITY AGAIN. THAT'S ALWAYS FUN.

BUT NO WORRIES, BECAUSE YOU HAVE A SYSTEM! IF YOU JUST GIVE UP CABLE AND THE INTERNET AND THE PHONE BILL AND PERHAPS ALL FORMS OF COMMUNICATION FOR THE MONTH, YOU CAN AFFORD TO USE YOUR STOVE AGAIN. OH, DID A BLACKOUT JUST WIPE OUT THE ENTIRE NEIGHBORHOOD? YOU GOT THIS. YOU GOT CANDLES AND MATCHES AND SHIT. YOU'VE WATCHED ENOUGH ZOMBIE APOCALYPSE MOVIES TO KNOW HOW TO SURVIVE LIKE THE PIONEERS USED TO, UNLIKE THE RICH FOLKS... WHO PROBABLY HAVE A SPARE GENERATOR AND HAVEN'T EVEN NOTICED THE WORLD IS ENDING. CURSE THEM.

==OH NO... AN OVERDRAFT FEE HAS PUT YOUR BANK ACCOUNT INTO NEGATIVE DOLLARS. BUT YOU MUST BE STRONG.==
==*Don't let them see you cry.*==

BE STRONG

NOTHING LIKE HAVING TO LITERALLY PAY THE PRICE FOR BEING POOR—ONLY TO BECOME POORER. HAVING "NEGATIVE DOLLARS" SHOULD NOT EVEN BE POSSIBLE, LET ALONE LEGAL, BUT CONSIDER YOURSELF AN OVERACHIEVER IN THE LEVELS OF POVERTY. IT'S OKAY, BUDDY. EVENTUALLY THEY CAN'T TAKE WHAT YOU DON'T HAVE, RIGHT?

UNLESS IT'S APRIL.

THE THINGS YOU DO FOR MONEY...

TAXES

27

…you don't want to talk about it.

THE THINGS YOU DO FOR MONEY...

==YOU HAVE HONESTLY CONSIDERED TRYING TO GO OFF THE GRID TO AVOID DEBT COLLECTORS.==

IT WOULDN'T EVEN BE THAT HARD. YOU KNOW A GUY WHO KNOWS A GUY WHO MIGHT KNOW HOW YOU CAN FAKE YOUR OWN DEATH. YOU'LL MOVE TO SOME REMOTE ISLAND IN THE PACIFIC, GET A NEW NAME, LIVE A SIMPLE LIFE—YOU COULD HAVE IT ALL. THAT IS, UNTIL THE FBI FINDS YOU AND ARRESTS YOU AND OH MAN, THIS WAS A TERRIBLE PLAN—ABORT MISSION, ABORT, *ABORT!*

retirement plans?
HA! YOU HAVE NO FUTURE.

HONESTLY, YOU DON'T EVEN KNOW HOW YOU'RE GOING TO PAY FOR THE RENT A MONTH FROM NOW, LET ALONE FIGURE OUT WHAT YOU'RE GOING TO BE DOING WHEN YOU'RE 62. WHO KNOWS, MAYBE YOU'LL BE DEAD. THE WORLD IS CRAZY AND CHAOTIC WHEN YOU DON'T HAVE "FINANCIAL SECURITY."

TO DO List

- ☐ Move to Florida.
- ☐ Take crocheting classes
- ☐ Sleep
- ☐ Go Sky Diving
- ☐ Take care of Grandchildren.

FEAR & LOATHING OUTSIDE THE WORKPLACE

THE ONE-PERCENTERS LIVE A LAVISH LIFE, DON'T THEY? SHOPPING IN PARIS, DANCING IN MADRID, NETWORKING IN TOKYO—THEY'RE TRAVELING ALL OVER THE WORLD, EXPERIENCING ANY CITY OF THEIR WILDEST DESIRES. MEANWHILE, THE ONLY TRAVELING YOU'RE DOING IS COMMUTING BACK AND FORTH FROM WORK EVERY DAY.

IF YOUR "VACATIONS" CONSIST OF MORE NETFLIX-BINGING AND LESS SUNBATHING IN HAWAII, THEN COME JOIN THE REST OF THE 99% IN RUSH HOUR LIMBO.

FEAR & LOATHING OUTSIDE THE WORKPLACE

YOU'VE LEARNED SOME SERIOUS LIFE LESSONS ON THE BUS.

WHAT IS IT ABOUT THE BUS/SUBWAY THAT BRINGS OUT THE CRAZY IN PEOPLE? ONE-PERCENTERS DON'T HAVE TO DEAL WITH DRUNK HOBOS RANTING IN THE BACK ABOUT THE IMPENDING APOCALYPSE OR HAVE TO BREAK OUT THE GYMNASTIC SKILLS IN ORDER TO GET PAST THE MOTHER WHO THOUGHT BRINGING A HUGE BABY CARRIAGE ON THE BUS WAS OKAY. YOU'VE LEARNED THE FINE SKILL OF EXAMINING THE SEATING AREA IN 2.5 SECONDS AND KNOWING WHO *NOT* TO SIT NEXT TO.

SCHEDULES MEAN NOTHING IN THE PUBLIC TRANSIT WORLD, SO YOU'VE GOT SOME TRUST ISSUES WITH TIME. IT'S FRUSTRATING HOW LONG COMMUTING IS WHEN YOU KNOW IT'D BE SO MUCH QUICKER IF YOU HAD A CAR. WHEN YOU GET A CAR, IT'LL BE BEAUTIFUL. THE WORLD WILL BE A GREAT PLACE.

OH NO!
YOU'RE ON THE WRONG BUS, YOU'RE GOING TO PAGE 42

YOUR PASSPORT IS VIRTUALLY USELESS.

DO YOU EVEN KNOW WHAT IT LOOKS LIKE? DO... DO YOU EVEN HAVE ONE?

MOST PEOPLE BARELY FLY OUT OF THE STATE, MUCH LESS THE COUNTRY, UNLESS THEY HAVE FAMILY TO VISIT. WHILE SOME ONE-PERCENTERS PROBABLY GET NEW PASSPORTS EVERY OTHER YEAR FROM FILLING THEIR BOOKLETS WITH ALL SORTS OF VISA STAMPS, YOU MIGHT JUST HAVE THE ONE OR TWO STAMPS IN ALL TEN YEARS YOU'VE OWNED YOUR PASSPORT BEFORE HAVING TO RENEW. BUT IT'S OKAY. THERE ARE PLENTY OF LOCAL PLACES TO VACAY AT INSIDE THE COUNTRY, RIGHT?

FINALLY.
HIT THE BEACH ON THE NEXT PAGE.

FEAR & LOATHING OUTSIDE THE WORKPLACE

NO MATTER WHERE YOU GO, THERE'S NO AVOIDING THE TOURISTS.

HOW SOMEONE CAN OWN AN ENTIRE PRIVATE BEACH ALL TO THEMSELVES, YOU'LL NEVER KNOW, AS YOU DESPERATELY TRY TO FIND A SPOT ON THE BEACH SAND AMONGST THE PACK OF TOURISTS. WHETHER YOU HAVE TO DEAL WITH SCREAMING CHILDREN THROWING SAND AND BEACH BALLS OR FACE THE HORROR THAT IS WATCHING HAIRY OLD MEN PARADE AROUND IN TEENY TINY SPEEDOS, YOUR SMALL HOPE OF GETTING A TAN WHILE RELAXING WITH A SUMMER NOVEL IS SHOT.

NO ONE CAN ESCAPE THE TOURISTS. THEY'RE IN ALL THE MUSEUMS, ALL THE SHOPPING DISTRICTS, ALL THE RESTAURANT NOOKS FEATURED IN TRAVELING SHOWS AND NEWSPAPER COLUMNS—THEY'RE EVERYWHERE. HOW DO THE CELEBRITIES AND WEALTHY ALIKE AVOID THIS MADNESS? CAN THEY PAUSE TIME AND ENJOY EVERY WORLDLY DESTINATION AT THEIR LEISURE? DO THEY HAVE INVISIBILITY CLOAKS? ARE THEY GODS? HOW? <u>HOW?</u>

HOW TO SPOT AN OLD MAN TOURIST

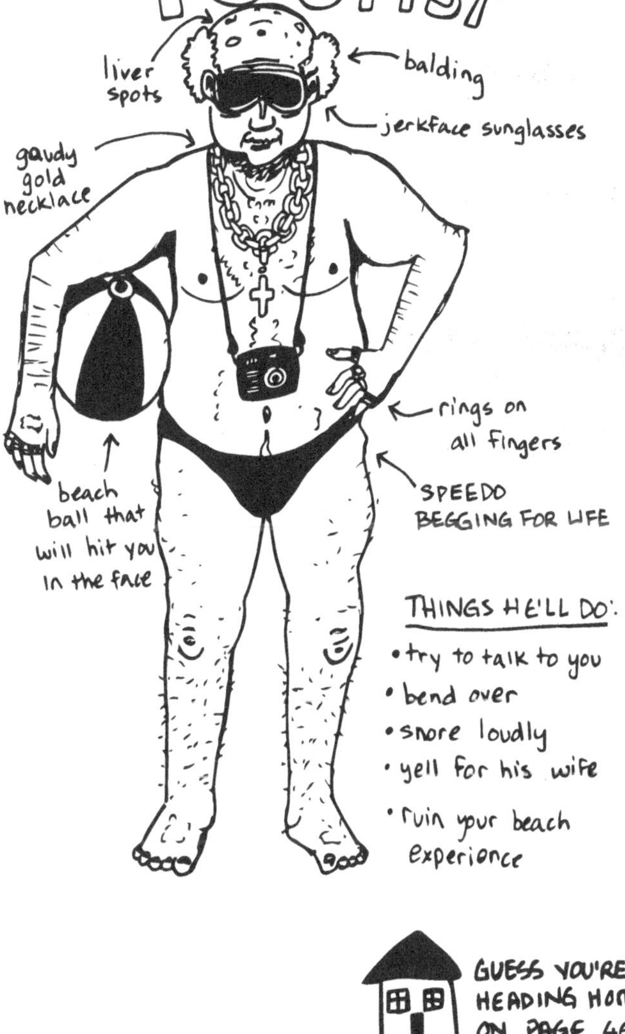

- liver spots
- balding
- jerkface sunglasses
- gaudy gold necklace
- beach ball that will hit you in the face
- rings on all fingers
- SPEEDO BEGGING FOR LIFE

THINGS HE'LL DO:
- try to talk to you
- bend over
- snore loudly
- yell for his wife
- ruin your beach experience

GUESS YOU'RE HEADING HOME ON PAGE 46.

FEAR & LOATHING OUTSIDE THE WORKPLACE

FINDING A PARKING SPOT AGAINST ALL ODDS IS LIKE WINNING IN THE OLYMPICS.

Unless you've got a parking spot with your name on it, chances are you're like the rest of us plebeians searching for salvation in the parking lot. Truly, it is a test of will, as you trudge up and down the lanes on the quest for a decent spot, always wondering if it's worth just parking in the back and walking the same five minutes it would take you to find one up close to the building. But why get exercise when you could have pride?

AND THERE IS NO GREATER GLORY THAN WINNING A PARKING JOUST. YOU PUT ON YOUR BLINKER TO CLAIM A SPOT AND YOUR OPPONENT ALSO PUTS ON HIS BLINKER TO CLAIM THE SPOT, BUT WHICH ONE OF YOU WILL CAVE FIRST? WHO WILL BE THE CHAMPION OF THE LOT? WHO WILL REIGN SUPREME AMONGST THE MASSES?

NOT YOU. IT'S JUST A PARKING SPOT, BUDDY. CALM DOWN. STOP CACKLING.

MAYBE THERE'S A PARKING SPOT ON PAGE 40?

FEAR & LOATHING OUTSIDE THE WORKPLACE

FLIGHT TICKET PRICES MOCK YOU.

You've researched all the ways to find cheaper airline tickets, whether it's scheduling trips around Tuesday mornings or keeping an eye on tourist season for a particular destination. You'll suck it up and choose the seats all the way in the back of the plane if it means saving $20, and you'll travel at four in the morning—you don't even care anymore—especially if it means saving $200 bucks. But even with all your efforts, plane flights are mad expensive, man.

And that's not even including the luggage fees, the carry-on fees, the other flight fees, the taxes, your arm, your leg, the soul of your first-born, a spare kidney...

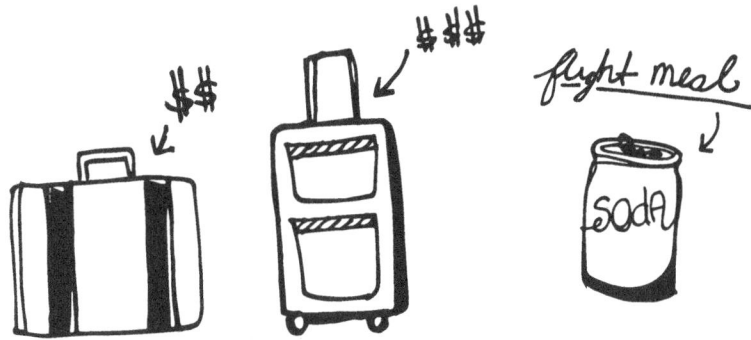

$$
\begin{array}{l}
\text{\$\$} \rightarrow \text{suitcase} \\
\text{\$\$\$} \rightarrow \text{carry-on} \\
\text{flight meal} \rightarrow \text{soda}
\end{array}
$$

SOME AIRLINE ☹	
CLASS: POOR AS HELL / STORAGE COMPARTMENT	SEAT + CLASS: 362
FLIGHT + DATE: FU 24/12	GATE: OTHER SIDE OF AIRPORT
BOARDING TIME: 3 HOURS DELAY, 4AM	
FROM: YOUR SHITTY HOME	TO: YOUR PARENTS' HOUSE (HELL)
	REMARKS: YOU AIN'T NEVER GETTING ON THE PLANE

BOARDING PASS

YOU NEED TO GO THROUGH CUSTOMS ON PAGE 33 ➡

FEAR & LOATHING OUTSIDE THE WORKPLACE

YOU HAVE REACHED A DARK PLACE
since you began commuting by car.

IN SHORT, YOU WANT TO KILL EVERYONE. YOU DIDN'T EVEN KNOW YOU POSSESSED A FIERY RAGE STRONGER THAN SATAN HIMSELF UNTIL 5PM ROLLED AROUND AND YOU FOUND YOURSELF STOPPED DEAD IN YOUR TRACKS ON THE HIGHWAY. THE THINGS YOU HAVE YELLED AT STRANGERS FROM THE CONFINES OF YOUR VEHICLE WOULD SHAME ALL OF YOUR ANCESTORS. YOU WILL PROBABLY HAVE TO CONSUME AN ENTIRE SOAP FACTORY TO CLEANSE YOURSELF OF YOUR FURY.

IT'S AS IF TIME GOES INTO SLOW MOTION DURING RUSH HOUR TRAFFIC, AND WHEN YOU GLANCE OVER TO YOUR LEFT TO YOUR NEIGHBOR WHO'S ALSO SCREAMING TO THE SKIES IN AGONY, AT LEAST YOU KNOW YOU'RE NOT ALONE. YOU'RE ALL HATING EACH OTHER TOGETHER.

welp. you're backtracking to page 36 for work today...

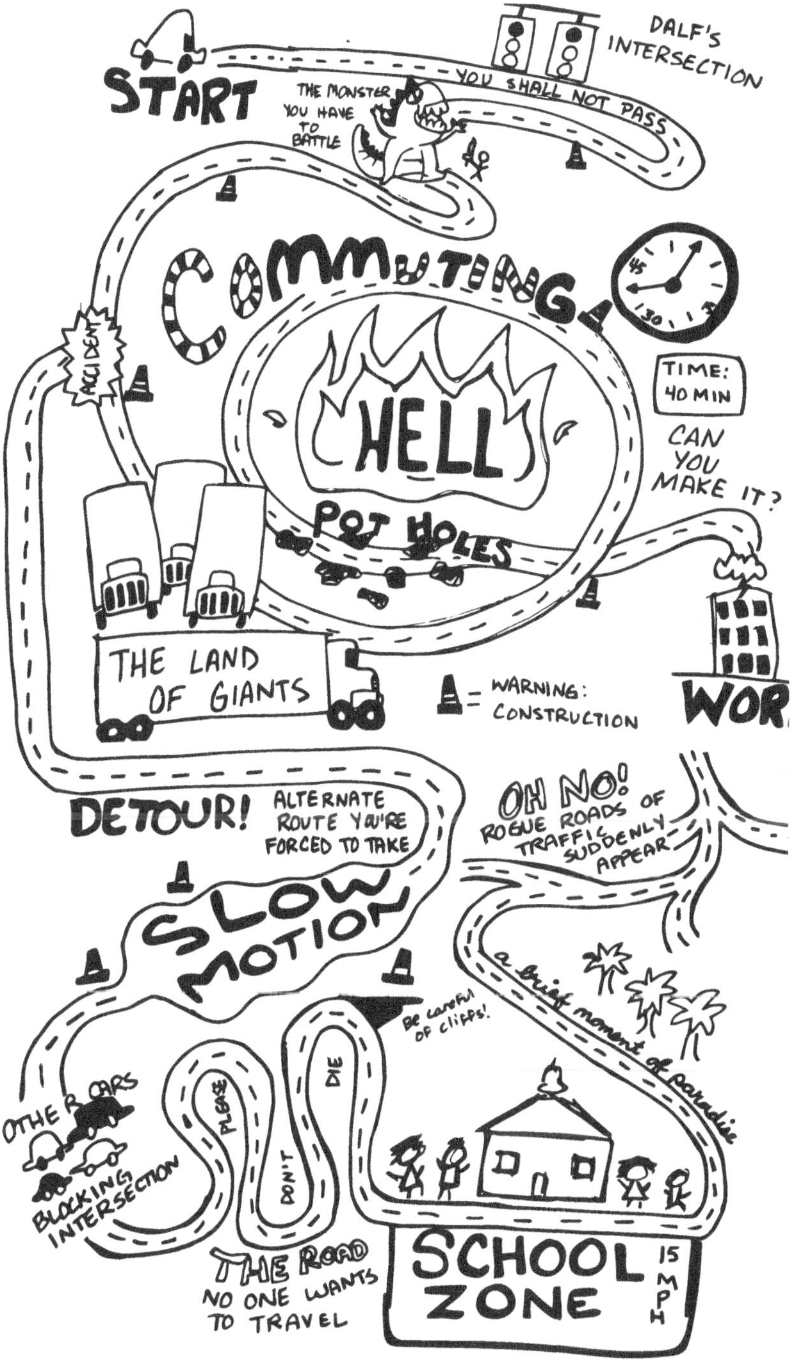
START
DALF'S INTERSECTION
YOU SHALL NOT PASS
THE MONSTER YOU HAVE TO BATTLE
COMMUTING
HELL
TIME: 40 MIN
CAN YOU MAKE IT?
ACCIDENT
POT HOLES
THE LAND OF GIANTS
= WARNING: CONSTRUCTION
WOR
DETOUR!
ALTERNATE ROUTE YOU'RE FORCED TO TAKE
OH NO! ROGUE ROADS OF TRAFFIC SUDDENLY APPEAR
SLOW MOTION
Be careful of cliffs!
a brief moment of paradise
OTHER CARS
BLOCKING INTERSECTION
PLEASE
DON'T
DIE
THE ROAD NO ONE WANTS TO TRAVEL
SCHOOL ZONE
15 MPH

FEAR & LOATHING OUTSIDE THE WORKPLACE

MONEY IS GAS IS MONEY.

WITH THE AMOUNT OF MONEY YOU'VE SPENT ON GAS TO GET TO AND FROM WORK, YOU COULD HAVE TRAVELED THE WORLD TEN TIMES OVER, AND THIS HURTS YOUR SOUL. POLITICS ASIDE, GAS PRICES ARE A CONSPIRACY—YOU JUST KNOW IT AND NO ONE CAN CONVINCE YOU OTHERWISE—WHAT WITH THEIR FLUCTUATING PRICES, TOYING WITH YOUR HEART ON A DAILY BASIS. GAS IS SOMETHING YOU WISH YOU COULD QUIT. YOU'RE TIRED OF THIS ONE-SIDED RELATIONSHIP!

SOME PEOPLE FOLLOW STOCKS ON WALL STREET WHILE YOU FOLLOW GAS PRICES AS YOU DRIVE DOWN THE STREET. WHATEVER THE GAS PRICE GODS WANT, YOU'D GIVE THEM IF YOU KNEW.

ASKING FOR VACATION TIME IS THE OFFICE'S BATTLE ROYALE.

SO YOU FINALLY SAVED UP SOME MONEY TO GO ON VACATION. GOOD LUCK GETTING THE TIME OFF FROM WORK, PAL. YOU CAN'T JUST GO OFF JET-SETTING ALL WILLY-NILLY, TAKING OFF SIX MONTHS TO "EXPLORE YOURSELF" LIKE THE WEALTHY DO. YOU GET MAYBE TWO WEEKS, AFTER WORKING LIKE TWO YEARS STRAIGHT, AND IF YOU'RE TRYING TO TAKE OFF TIME DURING THE HOLIDAYS, PREPARE YOURSELF FOR THE BLOODBATH ABOUT TO GO DOWN AT HUMAN RESOURCES.

BUT WHERE THERE'S A WILL, THERE'S A WAY, AND AIN'T NO ONE TAKING AWAY YOUR HOLIDAY.

Yay! YOU GOT YOUR VACATION. TIME TO GO TO PAGE 45

FEAR & LOATHING OUTSIDE THE WORKPLACE

Your vacations consist of catching up on errands, chores, & sleep. Not lying on the beach in Maui

The fact that on at least a few of your vacations, you looked forward to getting your car fixed, finally finding time to get a new mattress, and sleeping for three days straight on that mattress is a little concerning. If vacations amount to nothing more than an extended weekend—when you find time to binge-watch every season of some crime show drama on Netflix—then maybe it's time to reevaluate life a little.

You won't be able to drop everything and head for Costa Rica to an exotic beach resort, but all your hard work deserves some sort of getaway. Treat yo'self.

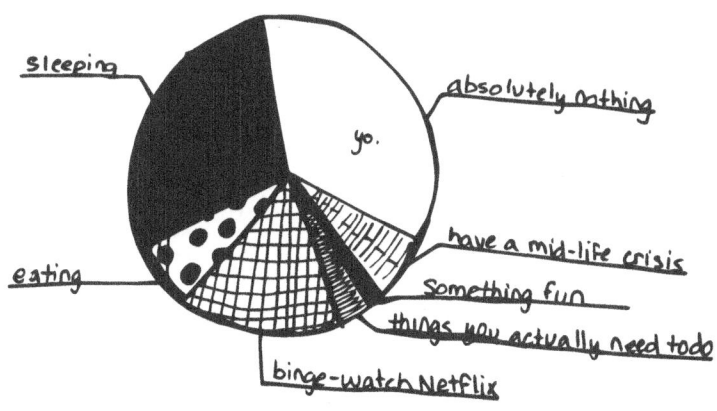

THINGS YOU DO ON VACATION
- sleeping
- absolutely nothing
- yo.
- eating
- have a mid-life crisis
- something fun
- things you actually need to do
- binge-watch Netflix

To Do List //

- ☐ Sleep
- ☐ EAT
- ☐ Catch up on latest show
- ☐ Breathe
- ☐ Work out for 20 minutes
- ☐ Finally clean up bedroom
- ☐ Fold pile of clothes you washed ONE MONTH AGO !!!

SHIT! YOU'RE ABOUT TO MISS YOUR FLIGHT! GO TO PAGE 39 **NOW.**

FEAR & LOATHING OUTSIDE THE WORKPLACE

AH, THE COMMUNITY POOL, WHERE SANITATION GOES TO DIE.

ALL YOU WANT IS A PLACE TO RELAX, AND THE COMMUNITY POOL IS NOT WHERE YOU'RE GOING TO FIND IT. YOU RUN INTO THE SAME ISSUES THAT YOU WOULD WITH TOURISTIC BEACH SPOTS: CHILDREN CANNONBALLING EVERYWHERE, OLD PEOPLE DIPPED IN SUNTAN LOTION BLINDING YOU, THAT CREEPY GUY WHO KEEPS STARING AT EVERYONE. ONLY HERE, PEOPLE JUDGE YOU. A LOVING COMMUNITY, THEY ARE.

HOME IS WHAT THE WALLET CAN AFFORD

WHEN YOU'RE IN THE TOP 1%, YOU CAN AFFORD TO LIVE WHEREVER YOU FEEL LIKE, WHETHER IT'S A PENTHOUSE IN A NEW YORK SKYSCRAPER OR A PRIVATE BEACH HOUSE IN MALIBU. THERE ARE NO LIMITS TO WHAT YOU CAN CALL HOME. YOU MIGHT EVEN GET AWAY WITH WALKING INTO SOMEONE ELSE'S HOUSE AND JUST CLAIMING IT YOURS. WITH ALL THE MONEY YOU HAVE, WHO COULD REALLY STOP YOU?

BUT THAT'S NOT YOU—NOT BECAUSE YOU'RE A GOOD PERSON, BUT BECAUSE YOU DON'T HAVE THAT KIND OF FINANCIAL FREEDOM. IT TOOK EVERYTHING YOU HAD TO BE ABLE TO AFFORD THE LITTLE AMOUNT OF CUBIC SPACE YOU CALL HOME, AND THESE NEXT FEW SIGNS MIGHT JUST REMIND YOU OF YOUR LOVELY ABODE.

HOME IS WHAT THE WALLET CAN AFFORD

FIRST OFF, YOU DON'T LIVE IN A :GATED COMMUNITY:

No one cares about your house, man. If you want peace and quiet in your neighborhood, you make like the rest of the hermit crabs in the world, and choose a dead-end part of the neighborhood. Otherwise, you'll just have to deal with beer bottles breaking in the street for ***West Side Story*** gang fights outside your window and couples on the verge of breakup fighting on the sidewalk. The only maintenance being done is you screaming at kids to get off your lawn, even when you don't have one.

And if you do, by some struck of luck, have a gate door to pass through before entering your neighborhood, it ain't all fancy and you know it. Just some automated machine that any thief could walk on by if he felt like it. Without a security guard, the neighbors might as well make the best of their situation and make a kickstarter to try to turn the gate pole into an Indiana Jones-style obstacle course. Keep everyone safe, you know?

THE ONLY SECURITY SYSTEM YOU HAVE IS YOUR PET DOG.

Some of those security alarm systems cost like a whopping $500, not including the monthly service fees. Live life on the edge, knowing someone out there might be out to steal your Nutri-Ninja blender. Anything of actual value you could just keep in a safe or a box under your mattress, like they did in pioneer times. Otherwise, it's up to your little four-legged creature to guard the house, assuming they don't befriend any intruders along the way. Sigh.

HOME IS WHAT THE WALLET CAN AFFORD

==THERE IS NO ELEVATOR TO YOUR PENTHOUSE DOOR. THERE IS NO ELEVATOR IN GENERAL.==

ELEVATORS ARE FOR WEAKLINGS.

TAKE THE STAIRS, MY FRIEND. GET THAT DAILY EXERCISE INTO YOUR ROUTINE. GOOD FOR YOUR LUNGS; GOOD FOR YOUR SOUL. FIVE FLIGHTS OF STAIRS IS PROBABLY JUST AS GOOD AS HAVING A STAIRMASTER 3000, SO SCREW THE CONVENIENCE ELEVATORS PROVIDE WHEN YOU'VE GOT A MAKESHIFT HEALTHY LIFESTYLE GOING ON. WHILE THE 1% ZOOM UP TO THEIR HOUSES VIA THE CLAUSTROPHOBIC DEATH TRAP, YOU'LL BE PUMPING IRON WITH EVERY BAG OF GROCERIES YOU LUG UP THE STAIRS. YOU'RE A CHAMPION, BABY. YOU'RE GONNA GO FAR!

STAIR MASTER
HARD
INTERMEDIATE
BEGINNER
BEGIN

CHOOSE YOUR LEVEL

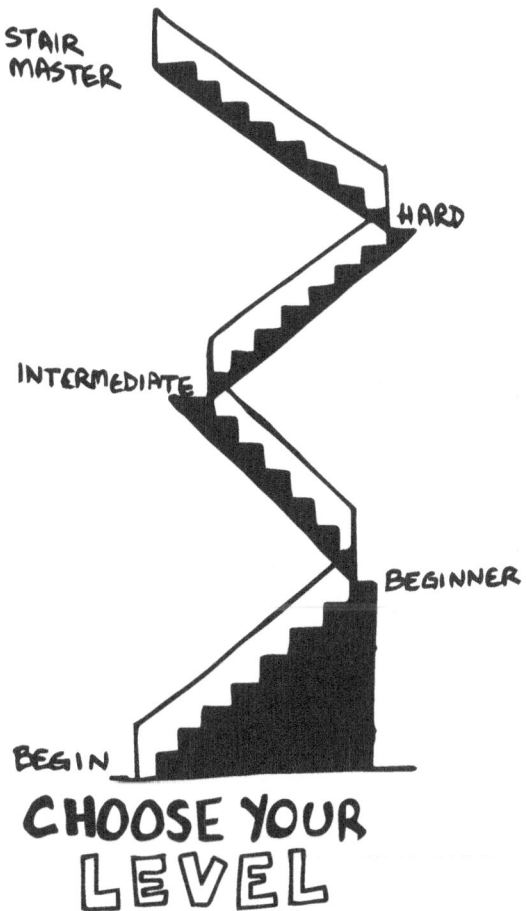

HOME IS WHAT THE WALLET CAN AFFORD

IT'S NOT LIKE YOU'RE TRYING TO EAVESDROP, BUT YOU, UH, KNOW THINGS ABOUT YOUR NEIGHBORS.

Nothing like some classy entertainment from beyond the wall to get you comfy on your couch. For every "I hate you; I wish you were dead" and uncomfortable, repetitive thumping against your bedroom wall, you wonder if maybe all apartments are designed to have paper-thin walls to have every sound echo across your house and haunt you for the rest of your life.

It's become increasingly hard looking your neighbors in the eye, knowing what they say, do, and listen to. You know that one guy above you is really into Korean pop girl bands and the elderly couple next door marathon *Breaking Bad* every day, six hours straight, and to be honest, you're kind of worried about them.

NIGHT

hello!

55

WHY DON'T YOU CALL YOUR MOTHER?

NOOO

PUT YOUR HANDS UP IN THE AIR

I HATE YOU!

I WISH YOU WERE DEAD

OOOH

Yes! Yes!

stop

YOU SHOULD BE MORE CAREFUL.

whaaaa!!!

PLEASE

I LOVE YOU

hi!

FINE, I DON'T NEED YOU ANYWAY

LET'S BUILD A POOL

GIVE IT TO ME!!!

HOME IS WHAT THE WALLET CAN AFFORD

YOU HAVE THE INTERIOR DESIGN AESTHETIC OF A DERANGED, REHABILITATED HOARDER.

YOU NEED TO GET YOUR SHIT TOGETHER, MAN.

SERIOUSLY, IT'S ALL OVER THE PLACE. BOOKS AND MAGAZINES EVERYWHERE, CLOTHES PILED UP ON THE FLOOR, WEIRD GIFTS YOU GOT FROM FRIENDS OVER THE YEARS SCATTERED IN NOOKS AND CRANNIES OF YOUR FURNITURE LAYOUT. LET'S FACE IT, BUYING A MATCHING LIVING ROOM SET IS A BIG DEAL IN YOUR WORLD THAT YOU MAY NOT BE READY FOR, SO YOU'RE STUCK WITH THE COUCH YOU GOT FROM GRANDMA, FURNITURE YOU PICKED UP OFF THE STREET DURING COLLEGE CHRISTMAS IN SEPTEMBER, AND STUFF YOU BOUGHT IN THE CLEARANCE RACK OF TARGET AND T.J.MAXX. YOU COULD ALWAYS GO TO IKEA AND PRETEND YOU LIVE THERE.

AM I A HOARDER?
(check yes if applicable)

- ☐ Shit is everywhere; laundry, bags, shoes...
- ☐ Frequently asks self, "Is it lost or stolen?"
- ☐ I do not remember what the floor looks like. I levitate to my bed.
- ☐ TLC asked to feature me.
- ☐ Not sure if pet ran away or is trapped inside the house.
- ☐ It's probably fine.
- ☐ I don't have a problem.
- ☐ I DON'T.

HOME IS WHAT THE WALLET CAN AFFORD

THE TOWELS IN YOUR BATHROOM MIGHT HAVE BEEN STOLEN FROM A HOTEL. AND THE SOAP. AND THE SHAMPOO. AND EVERYTHING ELSE THAT'S IN THE BATHROOM.

THE HOTEL IS GOING TO CHARGE YOU A "RESTOCKING" FEE ANYWAY, SO IT'S LIKE YOU PAID FOR IT ALREADY.

IF YOU HAVE NICE BATH PRODUCTS, YOU PROBABLY GOT THEM AS GIFTS FROM COWORKERS WHO DIDN'T KNOW WHAT TO GET YOU FOR CHRISTMAS OR YOUR BIRTHDAY. AND TO BE HONEST, YOU'RE OKAY WITH THAT. THOSE GIFTS FUEL YOUR SHOWERING HABITS. YOU'LL DEAL WITH SMELLING LIKE OVERRIPE PAPAYA FOR A FEW MONTHS UNTIL YOU GET YOUR NEXT BATCH OF BATHING GOODS, IF IT MEANS SAVING A TRIP TO THE PHARMACY STORE. NO ONE HAS TO KNOW WHERE YOU GET YOUR STUFF, MAN. SHHHH.

THINGS THAT ARE A-OKAY to STEAL

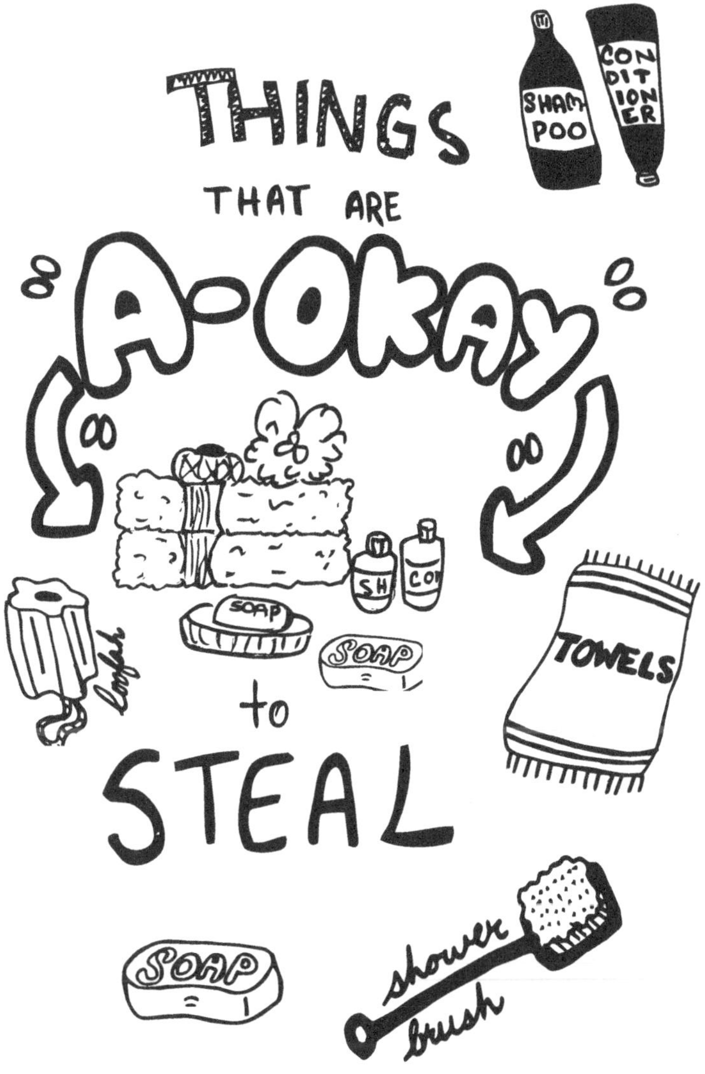
SHAMPOO
CONDITIONER
SH
CON
SOAP
SOAP
loofah
TOWELS
SOAP
shower brush

HOME IS WHAT THE WALLET CAN AFFORD

DUCT TAPE IS YOUR ONLY REPAIR SOLUTION.

YOUR MAINTENANCE STAFF IS A ROLL OF SILVER DUCT TAPE, A PRAYER, AND SWEET DENIAL. IT'S... OKAY. (IT'S NOT OKAY.) MOST OF US HAVE DECADES-OLD APPLIANCES HANGING ON A THREAD IN OUR HOUSES AND NO MONEY TO FIX THEM, SO NO NEED TO FEEL ASHAMED IN FRONT OF CERTAIN SOMEBODIES.

"JUST GO BUY A NEW ONE," THE ONE-PERCENTERS SAY AS THEY THROW OUT THEIR YEAR-OLD AIR CONDITIONING UNIT BECAUSE THE FILTER'S DIRTY. SOLID ADVICE.

YOU TRUST NO ONE IN THE REPAIR MAINTENANCE INDUSTRY. NO ONE.

IT'S A DIRTY WORLD OUT THERE, MUCH LIKE YOUR PLUMBING LAYOUT. EVERYONE KNOWS THE REPAIR MAINTENANCE INDUSTRY IS FULL OF SCAMS, WITH EVIL DOERS OUT TO DRAIN YOUR WALLET FOR ALL ITS WORTH. EVEN WHEN YOU HAVE INSURANCE AND THE REPAIR COSTS ARE COVERED, YOU SQUINT YOUR EYES AND QUESTION.

FACT IS, YOU'D TRUST YOURSELF MORE THAN A PERSON WHO WENT TO TRADE SCHOOL SPECIFICALLY TO FIX YOUR HOUSEHOLD APPLIANCES, WITH THE CERTIFICATIONS TO PROVE IT. HOW HARD COULD IT BE, RIGHT? IT'S NOT LIKE IT WOULD TAKE A FEW YEARS OF EXPERIENCE AND ON-HAND TRAINING TO FIX YOUR REFRIGERATOR. WITHIN THE HOUR, YOU'LL GET IT GOING AGAIN—OR HAVE WATER EXPLODING FROM THE BOTTOM, WHICHEVER. IT'S FINE.

FOR THE LOVE OF MONEY

You've sort of gotten your life together. You have a job, you have a house, and there's still the tiniest shred of hope that maybe there's someone out there for you. It's time to find a spouse, if only to reap all those tax benefits. Find someone who understands you, someone who will buy the food sometimes, someone who will split the rent. Ah, love—it's a dream!

While one-percenters rendezvous at ritzy bars and hotels, you and your sweet lover hit the two-for-one specials at restaurants. Life's easier when you've got a special someone to split the check with.

FOR THE LOVE OF MONEY

HONESTLY, YOU'RE JUST AIMING FOR A PARTNER WITH A JOB AT THIS POINT.

There's nothing sexier than financial security in this day and age. But you're not some gold digger trying to hop in a millionaire's lap (but you're not pushing them away either), instead just aiming for the bare minimum in a partner. Do they have a job? Yeah? Off to a great start.

Gone were the days where "money doesn't matter." Yeah, love's wonderful and all, but this ain't no romance drama, where the pauper meets their royal soul mate, okay. It's about teamwork, "I'll scratch your back if you scratch mine" kind of shit, making love after the bills are paid. Rejoice in your codependency!

WILL I GO OUT WITH YOU?

DO YOU HAVE A JOB?

YES → YES, I WILL GO ON A DATE WITH YOU.

NO → ARE YOU GOING to GET ONE SOON?

- YES! JUST GOT AN OFFER! → YES, I WILL GO ON A DATE WITH YOU.
- MAYBE → DEFINE "MAYBE"
- ...NO → ARE YOU EVEN TRYING?
  - YES, LIKE REALLY HARD → ARE YOU MODERATELY ATTRACTIVE?
    - HELL YEAH → MAYBE
    - UM... → MAYBE
  - NOT REALLY → THIS ISN'T GOING TO WORKOUT

FOR THE LOVE OF MONEY

THAT TIME YOU TRIED OUT ONLINE DATING WAS A DARK PERIOD IN YOUR LIFE, OKAY?

So, you were having some bad luck trying to find your mate and you resorted to online dating. It's alright. It's the twenty-first century. More people are doing it than they'd like to admit. Matchmaking services have been around for centuries, and putting them online isn't gonna make much of a difference.

Those a little more well off will actually have money to put into these algorithm machines, like eHarmony with their monthly service fees (uh, yeah right to spending money before you even land the date), while you opt for the totally-free OkCupid and Tinder, and enter the world of creeps and psychos at the swipe of a finger. With no actual screening process, you've experienced horror stories and now have a top 10 worst dates list that would shock the masses of what you'll endure for a free meal. You could have ***died.***

CHIVALRY MAKES YOUR BANK ACCOUNT DEAD. ONE OF YOU HAS TO BUY THE POPCORN AND SODA AT THE MOVIES.

IN THIS ECONOMY, EVERYONE IN THE 99% IS ALL ABOUT GOING DUTCH. EVERYONE'S EQUAL IN THE GAME OF LOVE. BECAUSE JEEZ, JUST GOING TO THE MOVIE THEATRE WILL DROP $22 ON TICKETS ALONE, NOT INCLUDING ANOTHER $20 IF YOU WANT THEATRE FOOD—BLESS YOUR SOUL IF YOU TRIED GOING OUT TO DINNER FIRST. THAT IS A LEVEL OF COMMITMENT THAT'S MARRIAGE-WORTHY, NOT A FIRST DATE.

FOR YOU AND YOUR LOVED ONE, YOU TRADE OFF DATE BILLS. IF THEY CAN'T HANDLE THIS SYSTEM, THEN GOOD RIDDANCE. IF THEY'RE LOOKING FOR A SUGAR DADDY/MOMMA, THEN THEY ARE IN FOR A ROUGH TIME.. BECAUSE THE FACT OF THE MATTER IS...

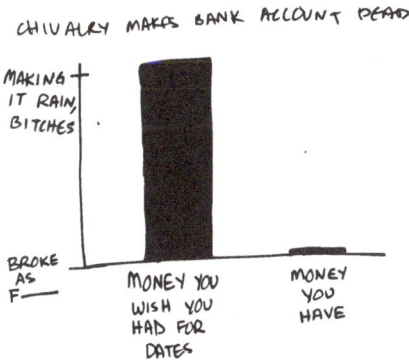

FOR THE LOVE OF MONEY

YOU'RE MORE WORRIED ABOUT FREE LOADERS THAN YOU ARE ABOUT GOLD DIGGERS.

YOU'RE NOT RICH ENOUGH TO HAVE GOLD DIGGERS, BUT YOU'RE STABLE ENOUGH TO HAVE A FREE LOADER SUCK THE LIFE OUT OF YOUR SAVINGS. AT SOME POINT EVERYONE HAS DEALT WITH THIS KIND OF EX: THE ONE WHO IMMEDIATELY ASKS FOR YOUR NETFLIX PASSWORD (THAT'S SERIOUS RELATIONSHIP LEVEL, BUDDY, YOU DON'T JUST HAND THAT OUT), WHO EATS ALL YOUR FOOD AND NEVER CHIPS IN FOR GROCERIES, WHO IS ALWAYS "RUNNING LOW ON GAS" AND EXPECTS YOU TO DRIVE EVERYWHERE. THEY'RE THE LEECH YOU'LL RESENT THE REST OF YOUR LIFE ONCE YOU'RE RID OF THEM.

IT'S NOT AS IF YOU DON'T PLAY WELL WITH OTHERS OR THAT YOU DON'T LOVE YOUR PARTNER, NO. WHEN YOU REALLY FIND THE OTHER HALF OF YOUR SOUL, THE YIN TO YOUR YANG, THE MAC TO YOUR CHEESE, THEN YOU'RE DEFINITELY ALL ABOUT MAKING THEM A PART OF YOUR LIFE. JUST MAYBE THEY COULD HELP PAY THE CABLE BILL, YOU KNOW?

GETTING A JOINT BANK ACCOUNT WAS A BIG DEAL IN YOUR RELATIONSHIP.

Some people daydream about a lavish engagement proposal, whereas you fantasize of the day you and your partner decide to get a joint bank account. It's kind of a big deal. Two people joining in an act of monetary love. You really see people's true colors when money's being shared. For the rich who don't have to worry about budgets, this doesn't even faze them, but for the rest of the 99%, the situation involves a lot more petty arguments on who spent the toilet paper money on a chicken clock that glows in the dark. Okay, like, maybe it's cool, but we needed toilet paper, babe.

If you're not the one worrying about maintaining the joint bank account, you're probably the one getting yelled at for running the well dry. It's not a magic pot of gold, buddy. Don't be that person.

FOR THE LOVE OF MONEY

YOUR WEDDING VENUE WAS A COMPILATION OF DIY PROJECTS YOU GOT OFF PINTEREST.

Planning a wedding is just a constant reminder of how microscopic the budget is when you're in the 99% crowd. It's a struggle. Busting out paper plates and plastic silverware, hand-making all of your centerpieces with a hot glue gun and some desperation, and debating whether it's worth potentially going to jail just to steal that $500 wedding cake from the bakery.

Still, for those trying to plan their wedding, thank the Pinterest gods for the infinite amount of budget-friendly, DIY projects on College Girls'"++Wedding For Future Ref <3!!++" boards to give you plenty of ideas of what to do for the big day. That is, if they don't fail on you. Eh, when in doubt, put everything in a mason jar. Just get a shit ton of mason jars. All the rage.

JARS.

MASON JAR MADNESS

Put everything in a mason jar. Just do it.

GIVE YOUR WEDDING A BARNHOUSE!!!

You won't regret this decision ever.

GROOMSMEN GIFT IDEAS HE'LL ACTUALLY USE!

– a cooler that doesn't cool shit

He'll never use any of this.

You should get to know your husband

Wedding INVITATIONS

SPRAY-PAINT A GIANT LETTER

Because why not?

YOU'LL NEVER AFFORD THIS WEDDING DRESS

But it's nice to dream.

101 INSANELY STUPID ♥ Wedding ♥ ☆ IDEAS ☆

Started out fun, then became a fire hazard.

We'll call 911 before anyone dies.

PLEASE SIGN *blank*

I ♥ U

WRITE SOMETHING STUPID ON A CHALK BOARD

It'll show love.

19 SPECTACULARLY NERDY, DIY WEDDING CAKES

CAUSE YOU NEED A DOCTOR WHO CAKE

To show people you're "nerdy"

Love & SHIT

Fall in love with your partner all over again

Otherwise, it will get awkward.

Doilies ✿ ✿ ✿ ✿

It's the only time you will ever use doilies, tbh.

And don't get the...

DIY

READ MORE

CANDLES. CANDLES DIY. CANDLES!!!!!

CANDLES 4 LYFE

HIS AND HERS EVERYTHING

~~his and hers~~

Because you need to start dividing stuff

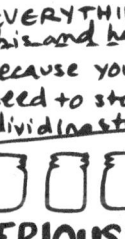
SERIOUSLY, JUST USE A ~shit ton~ of MASON JARS

It's so quirky and original.

Totes unique.

♥ **THIS LIST WILL PLAN THE WEDDING FOR** ♥

FOR THE LOVE OF MONEY

YOUR HONEYMOON ISN'T GOING TO BE AS EXOTIC AS YOU HOPED IT WOULD BE.

Couples surfing in Honolulu, gondola rides through Venice, tango dancing in Buenos Aires—yeeeah, most of us are doing none of this during our honeymoons. Like maybe you could get a Groupon deal for a 2-day cruise to the Bahamas, but otherwise, you're stuck at some bed and breakfast run by a cat lady in some remote location.

My friend, it's not where you go, but who you go with. While the wealthy may enjoy more adventurous activities, you can relax with your honey and smooch over overpriced cocktails at the poolside. Besides, honeymoons are about hotel rooms. For what you couldn't spend on an exotic trip, you kicked up the bed

NEITHER OF YOU IS GOING TO BE A TROPHY SPOUSE. NOT EVEN A RIBBON FOR PARTICIPATION.

YOU REALLY SHOULD GET A TROPHY FOR BEING MARRIED, THOUGH, WHAT WITH THE NEVER-ENDING LOAN TRIATHLON YOU BOTH HAVE TO ENDURE: STUDENT LOANS, CAR LOANS, MORTGAGE LOANS. THE IRS SHOULD AT THE VERY LEAST GIVE YOU SPORTS A RIBBON FOR NOT MURDERING EACH OTHER AS YOU BOTH TRY TO KEEP YOUR MARRIAGE ALIVE THROUGH FINANCIAL CRISES.

FOR THE LOVE OF MONEY

NO ONE MENTIONED A PRE-NUP. CAUSE WHY?

LIKE, WHAT DO YOU HAVE THAT YOU'RE WORRIED ABOUT LOSING? THE DOG? OKAY, MAYBE THAT ONE'S LEGITIMATE, BUT COME ON.

DIVORCE WAS MESSY, BUT IT WASN'T ALIMONY IN THE MILLIONS MESSY.

YOU DON'T HAVE MANY ADVANTAGES OVER THE TOP 1%, BUT YOU CAN SAFELY SAY DIVORCE WILL NEVER BE AS BAD AS WHAT THEY HAVE TO GO THROUGH. WHEN YOU GET A DIVORCE, YOU'RE NOT LOSING MILLIONS IN ALIMONY TO YOUR EX. MAYBE SOME FURNITURE (THAT WE BOUGHT TOGETHER, BABE), OR SOME AUTOGRAPHED POSTERS/ALBUMS, OR THE FAMILY PET (WHICH IS WHAT YOU'RE REALLY SAD ABOUT), BUT OTHERWISE, YOU'RE NOT INVOLVING AN ACCOUNTANT ALONG WITH YOUR DIVORCE LAWYER.

IT'S JUST EMOTIONAL DAMAGE AND CHILD CUSTODY BATTLES, LIKE THE REST OF US.

SETTLING DOWN INTO NOTHING

THE THINGS YOU DO FOR THE PURSUIT OF HAPPINESS—MY FRIEND, YOU DO NOT HAVE ENOUGH MONEY TO RAISE A PET, LET ALONE A FAMILY, AND YET THERE YOU GO OFF, REPRODUCING AND CONTRIBUTING TO THE GENE POOL. YOU LOOKED AT YOUR BANK ACCOUNT AND THEN AT BABY CLOTHES, AND THOUGHT, "CHALLENGE ACCEPTED". YOU DON'T KNOW HOW YOU MANAGE TO RAISE ENOUGH MONEY TO FEED THE LITTLE MEAT BODIES EVERY DAY, BUT YOU'RE JUST THANKFUL YOU'VE GOTTEN THIS FAR.

SETTLING DOWN INTO NOTHING

PROBABLY STILL GETTING JUST $5 FROM YOUR GRANDPARENTS ON YOUR BIRTHDAY, AREN'T YOU?

YOU COULD BE TEN, YOU COULD BE FORTY-FIVE—YOU'RE STILL GETTING AN ABRAHAM LINCOLN FROM GRANDMA, SO YOU BETTER USE IT WISELY. MAYBE AT ONE POINT IN HER LIFE, FIVE DOLLARS COULD HAVE AFFORDED A BRAND NEW TELEVISION OR SOMETHING, YOU DON'T KNOW, BUT NOW IT'S JUST A SAD REMINDER THAT TIMES HAVE CHANGED AND THAT ACTUALLY, YOU STILL NEED ANOTHER DOLLAR FOR A COMBO MEAL AT BURGER KING.

You know the humiliation that comes with asking your parents for money or moving back home.

You don't want to do it, you really don't. Asking your parents for money or moving back home is admitting defeat in this capitalistic society. Sure, they're supposed to help you out in life because you're their child or whatever, but it always leaves a bad taste in your mouth knowing your parents had to pay your rent this month.

Unlike the one-percent kids, who'd gladly ask for money from mommy and daddy, you have what is called "guilt," knowing you're taking hard-earned cash from your parents' paycheck. But it's okay, my friend. Every bird leaves the nest eventually, even if it takes a few times plunging straight into bankruptcy.

SETTLING DOWN INTO NOTHING

THE HAND-ME-DOWNS ARE SO OLD, THEY'RE PRACTICALLY THE FAMILY HEIRLOOMS.

THE ERA OF JEANS 1941

Great-grandpa **JOE** (the one who started it all)

Grandpa **JOE jr.**

Papa **J.J.**

FRANK

HOW MANY GENERATIONS HAVE WORN THAT SAME PAIR OF JEANS, MAN? THIS AIN'T NO SISTERHOOD OF THE TRAVELING PANTS—THE BELL BOTTOMS HAVE TO DIE.

WHEN YOU'VE GOT CLOTHES THAT DATE BACK TO THE GREAT DEPRESSION, IT IS TIME TO LET THEM GO. YOUR CHILD WILL THANK YOU FOR ENDING THE FASHION STRIKE AGAINST MODERN TIMES, GUARANTEED. NO ONE'S ASKING YOU TO GO CRAZY AND BUY SOME TOMMY HILFIGER JEANS, BUT COME ON, MAN, YOU CAN SPARE A FEW BUCKS FOR SOME PANTS. BEGIN A NEW ERA OF HAND-ME-DOWNS.

YOU SHARED TOYS, & SO WILL YOUR KIDS.

SOLOMON'S TEDDY

FOR THE MOST PART, YOU'RE NOT TRYING TO PIN YOUR KIDS AGAINST EACH OTHER. BUT WAS THE DEATH BATTLE FOR A TEDDY BEAR YOUR AFTERNOON ENTERTAINMENT? MAYBE.

SETTLING DOWN INTO NOTHING

THE MANY JOYS OF AN EMPTY BOX ARE LIMITLESS WITH ~IMAGINATION~.

WAS A GREAT MAJORITY OF YOUR CHILDHOOD SPENT ALONE IN A CARDBOARD BOX? THAT'S PROBABLY NORMAL.

IT'S ALWAYS A GOOD LIFE SKILL TO TEACH CHILDREN: THE ART OF IMAGINATION. WHY DEPRIVE YOUR CHILD OF EPIC BATTLES AND LOVE DRAMAS FUELED BY THE LITTLE THOUGHT NEURONS FLOATING THROUGH THEIR BRAINS WITH FANCY "REAL" TOYS WHEN YOU CAN GIVE THEM AN OBJECT—ANY OBJECT, LITERALLY ANYTHING—AND TELL THEM TO GO CRAZY, KID. MAKE THEM BELIEVE THEIR MINDS ARE GATEWAYS TO OTHER WORLDS. THEY ACTUALLY BELIEVE THAT SORT OF THING.

NO NANNIES FOR YOU.
LOOKS LIKE YOU'LL JUST HAVE TO RAISE YOUR KIDS.

WHAT A TRAGEDY, HAVING TO BUILD INTIMATE, LIFE-LASTING BONDS WITH THE BEINGS YOU PRODUCED. IT'S LIKE YOU LOVE THEM OR SOMETHING, LIKE YOU'D PROBABLY DO ANYTHING FOR THEM, LIKE YOU ACTUALLY WANTED THEM TO EXIST IN YOUR LIFE TO FILL SOME NURTURING DESIRE IN YOUR HEART—WEIRD. WHO DOES THAT? THE RICH DON'T. PARENTAL FIGURES ARE BUT MERE CONCEPTS FOR THE UPPER CLASS. ONLY PLEBEIANS ESTABLISH PSYCHOLOGICALLY ENHANCING RELATIONSHIPS WITH THEIR PARENTS.

...sometimes.

SETTLING DOWN INTO NOTHING

YOUR KID'S COLLEGE FUND REMAINS TO BE A COIN JAR ON TOP OF THE FRIDGE.

your kid could always get a scholarship, right?

HAVING SOUL-CRUSHING STUDENT LOAN DEBT IS A RITE OF PASSAGE NOWADAYS ANYWAY, SO DON'T FEEL BAD THAT ALL YOU'VE MANAGED TO SAVE FOR YOUR KID'S COLLEGE FUND WAS ENOUGH FOR ONE SEMESTER'S WORTH OF TEXTBOOKS. UNLESS YOUR KID HAS BUSTED SOME CHOPS TO GET SCHOLARSHIPS AND GRANTS OR RAN AWAY TO JOIN THE CIRCUS INSTEAD OF GOING TO COLLEGE, IT'S THE INEVITABLE DEFEAT-THE-DRAGON BATTLE THE REST OF THE 99% GOES THROUGH: STUDENT LOANS. ONLY SO FEW HAVE LIVED LONG ENOUGH TO TELL THE TALE.

YOU MAY **NOT HAVE A FANCY PUREBRED** DOG OR CAT, BUT AT LEAST YOUR PET IS A RESCUE YOU'RE LIKE A HERO

GOOD FOR YOU, BUDDY.
THAT'S IT. JUST FEEL GOOD ABOUT THIS. MAYBE GIVE YOUR PET A TREAT OR SOMETHING.

MEET:
RESCUE-OWNER MAN & CAT LADY

- they rescue animals from all over the world!
- they pick up animals from off the streets! (which is ill-advised, but they give the pets shots, so it's okay!)
- saving one animal at a time in shelters
  - everywhere -

SETTLING DOWN INTO NOTHING

FANCY FEAST? PEDIGREE? WHAT, YOUR PET THINKS IT HAS STANDARDS?

OKAY, BUT WHO DO THEY THINK THEY ARE?

YOUR CAT KILLS COCKROACHES FOR FUN. YOUR DOG EATS VOMIT OFF THE FLOOR. THERE WILL BE NO GRADE-A MEAT FOR YOUR FURRY LITTLE FRIENDS IF YOU'RE NOT EVEN DINING THAT FINE. SURE, MAYBE ONE DAY YOU'LL LIKE TO TREAT YOUR FELINE PAL TO THE FINEST SUSHI IN TOKYO AND GIVE SOME STATE-OF-THE-ART BONE MARROW TO YOUR CANINE FRIEND, BUT WITH YOUR BUDGET, THEY'RE JUST GETTING REGULAR CANNED FOOD AND BAGGED KIBBLES, LIKE THE REST OF THE FAMILY.

THERE WILL BE NO DIAMOND-STUDDED COLLARS OR LITTLE DESIGNER OUTFITS FOR YOUR FURRY LITTLE FRIENDS.

EVER SINCE PARIS HILTON DRESSED HER CHIHUAHUAS IN PINK TUTUS OR WHATEVER, IT'S AS IF THE WHOLE DOG COMMUNITY EXPLODED WITH ALL SORTS OF ATTIRE TO SHOVE YOUR RELUCTANT CANINE IN. AND GRANTED, IT'S ADORABLE, BUT YOUR LITTLE FLUFFBALL WON'T APPRECIATE A DOGGIE SWEATER DESIGNED BY VERSACE. AND DO YOU REALLY WANT TO LIVE WITH THE FACT THAT YOUR DOG MIGHT BE WEARING SOMETHING MORE EXPENSIVE THAN YOUR ENTIRE WARDROBE?

DO YOU WANT TO GIVE YOUR DOG THAT KIND OF POWER?

POPPING TAGS & CLIPPING COUPONS

MORE OFTEN THAN NOT, SHOPPING IS MISSION: IMPOSSIBLE, WHERE EVERY STORE YOU ENTER HAS SOME SORT OF GAME PLAN INVOLVING CLEARANCE SALES, DISCOUNT SPECIALS, AND MARKED TAGS. YOU LITERALLY HAVE BATTLE SCARS FROM YOUR SHOPPING EXCURSIONS, AND YOU CONSIDER SOME PRODUCTS VICTORY TROPHIES.

YOUR UNIQUE STYLE IS A RESULT OF FINDING PEARLS IN THE SALES RACK JUNKYARD, WHERE SOMETIMES YOU HIT THE JACKPOT AND OTHER TIMES YOU WONDER WHY ANYONE WOULD BUY A NEON GREEN LEOTARD SWEATER.

POPPING TAGS & CLIPPING COUPONS

YOU HAVE MASTERED THE ART OF HAGGLING, GRASSHOPPER. YOU'RE READY FOR THE FLEA MARKETS.

SHOPPING IS A MISSION, NOT A LEISURE ACTIVITY. WHEN YOU GO TO FLEA MARKETS, IT'S ABOUT DEFEATING YOUR MERCHANT OPPONENT AT HIS OWN GAME: HAGGLING. YOU'LL HAGGLE OVER SOMETHING THAT COSTS ONLY A DOLLAR, YOU DON'T CARE. YOU'LL FIGHT SOMEBODY. BRING IT.

HAVE YOU GONE SO FAR AS TO TRY TO HAGGLE DOWN A GIRL SCOUT? NO, MAYBE NOT, MAYBE. BUT YOU'RE NOT ABOUT TO LET YOUR GUARD DOWN AND YOU NEVER LIST YOUR PRICE FIRST. YOU'VE GOT THE FINE BUSINESS SKILLS THE TOP 1% HAVE, JUST ON A SMALLER, PERSONAL SCALE. TELL YOU WHAT, THOUGH. IF ANYONE EVEN TRIED TO SCAM YOU OUT OF A DOLLAR, THEY'D PROBABLY END UP GIVING YOU TWO.

THE PEOPLE ON EXTREME COUPONING ARE KIND OF YOUR IDOLS.

YOU CLIP COUPONS LIKE YOU'RE READING STOCK AVERAGES ON WALL STREET, ALWAYS ON THE LOOK FOR THE BEST DEALS IN THIS CAPITALISTIC WORLD. GOT COUPS? YEAH, YOU GOT COUPS. IF YOU'RE FANCY, YOU MIGHT EVEN HAVE A SPECIAL WALLET FOR YOUR COUPONS, ORGANIZED BY PRODUCT CATEGORY OR EXPIRATION DATE OR BOTH. BE HONEST, THE MAIN REASON YOU HAVE A NEWSPAPER SUBSCRIPTION IS FOR THE COUPONS.

MAYBE ONE DAY YOU'LL REACH SAVE-LEVEL HARDCORE AND HAVE THE GROCERY STORE OWE YOU MONEY BY THE END OF THE TRANSACTION, BUT FOR NOW, YOU SPEND YOUR DAYS FIGHTING AGAINST EXPIRATION DATES (IT'S STILL YESTERDAY IN ANOTHER TIME ZONE, RIGHT?—THAT'S HOW TIME WORKS) AND HOW MANY TIMES YOU CAN USE YOUR COUPON. GOTTA SAVE THAT MONEY.

POPPING TAGS & CLIPPING COUPONS

THRIFT STORE
IS THE BEST STORE!

You don't want to be a hipster about it, but uh, you've definitely been shopping at thrift stores before it was cool. Before neck-bearded twenty-somethings and nostalgia-core teens dominated the scene, you were popping tags and claiming names like it was nobody's business. You weren't in it for the trends, but the sweet deals. You've been rocking the frugal fashion way before Mackelmore donned recycled fur to rap about thrift shop treasures.

That's one thing you'll always have an upper hand on the one-percenters. If you want unique clothing that screams nothing but your personality, thrift store finds will deliver. While the wealthy may panic about who wears it better?, you can safely rock your second-hand outfit, knowing there won't be anyone this decade strutting in your style.

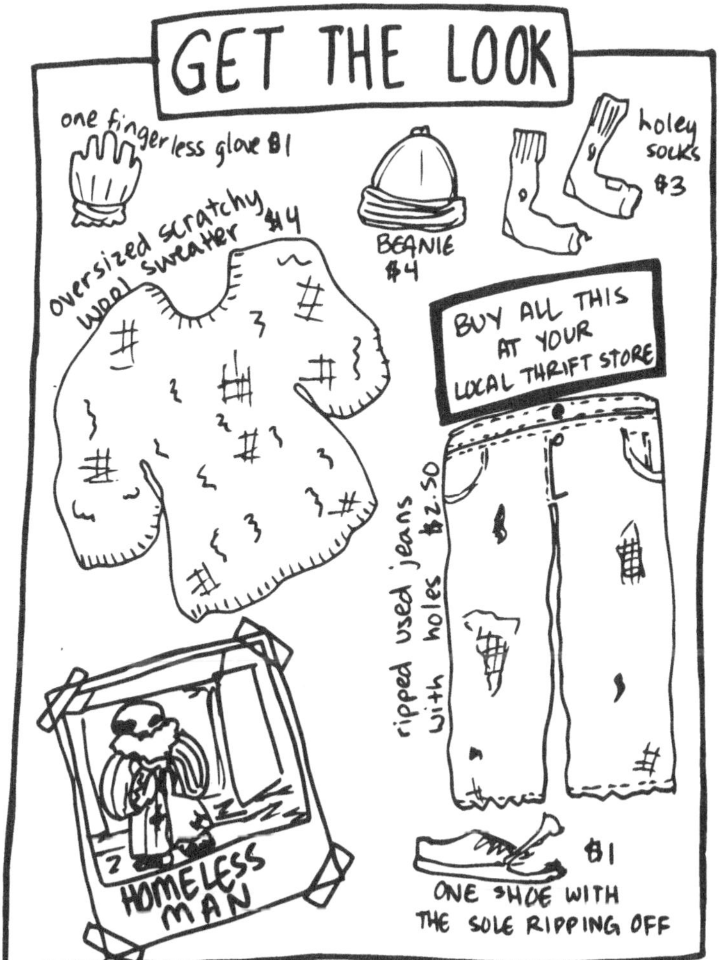
GET THE LOOK
one fingerless glove $1
BEANIE $4
holey socks $3
oversized scratchy wool sweater $14
BUY ALL THIS AT YOUR LOCAL THRIFT STORE
ripped used jeans with holes $2.50
HOMELESS MAN
$1
ONE SHOE WITH THE SOLE RIPPING OFF

POPPING TAGS & CLIPPING COUPONS

IT IS ACTUALLY DANGEROUS FOR YOU TO STEP INSIDE A TARGET.

LISTEN, SOME PEOPLE HAVE SHOPPING SPREES AT BLOOMINGDALE'S, BUT IF YOU'RE GOING TO HAVE A SHOPPING SPREE ANYWHERE, IT'S AT TARGET. AND YOU DIDN'T EVEN MEAN TO. YOU NEVER MEAN TO. YOU KEEP TELLING YOURSELF TO JUST GET IN AND GET OUT, BUT THEN YOU LOOK AT THE $1-ITEM SECTION, AND THEN YOU NOTICE THEY GOT SOCKS FOR $3 AND IT'S ALWAYS GOOD TO HAVE SOCKS, AND THEN HOLY SHIT, THEY'RE SELLING BASIC TEES FOR $5? IS THAT AN OWL-SHAPED TEA POT FOR $15? YOU DON'T EVEN DRINK MUCH TEA, BUT WITH THIS NEW TEAPOT, YOU'RE GONNA DAMN WELL START.

EVERY TIME YOU EVENTUALLY MAKE IT TO THE TARGET CASH REGISTERS, DROWNING IN THE SALES DEALS YOU FOUND, YOU HATE YOURSELF FOR FALLING VICTIM TO THE WITCHCRAFT YET AGAIN. WHY DID YOU EVEN TRY TO BROWSE, MAN? YOU NEVER BROWSE THROUGH TARGET. THEY KNOW YOU. THEY KNOW

YOUR AESTHETIC. YOU ARE THE LITERAL TARGET AUDIENCE. NICE STUFF AT A CHEAP PRICE? STRIKE AN ARROW THROUGH YOUR HEART, FOR YOU HAVE FALLEN.

CAN YOU ENTER THE **TARGET**

AND **ESCAPE?**

(the answer is no)

POPPING TAGS & CLIPPING COUPONS

YOU'VE BOUGHT underwear on sale.

TAKE ADVANTAGE OF THE 3-FOR-1 SALES AT VICTORIA'S SECRET AND SEARS LIKE THE REST OF US.

DRY CLEANERS

IF YOU NEED A REGULAR DRY CLEANER, THEN IT MEANS YOU ACTUALLY HAVE GOOD CLOTHES TO TAKE CARE OF, BUT HAS THERE EVER BEEN A DRY CLEANERS PLACE THAT DIDN'T LOOK LIKE A TIME CAPSULE TO THE GREAT DEPRESSION? TRULY, IF YOU WANT TO LEARN OF TIMES PAST, JUST STEP INSIDE THE DINGY PLACE WITH MISSING TILES OFF THE FLOOR, AND INHALE ALL THE FUMES TO YOUR HEART'S CONTENT WHILE LISTENING TO PLASTIC BAGS GET CAUGHT IN THE CLOTHES RACK MACHINE.

POPPING TAGS & CLIPPING COUPONS

SCORING A SALES DEAL CAN SOMETIMES *be a religious experience.*

THERE ARE PIECES IN YOUR CLOSET YOU CONSIDER LEGENDS: THE PANTS YOU BOUGHT FOR JUST TWO DOLLARS, THE DESIGNER SHIRT YOU FOUND TUCKED IN A CORNER AT A THRIFT STORE, FIVE-DOLLAR SHOES THAT HAVE LASTED YOU FOR FIVE YEARS. AND YOU'LL TELL THEIR STORIES UNTIL THE DAY YOU DIE.

YOU REMEMBER THE MOMENT YOU GASPED HOLY MACKEREL, WONDERING IS THIS REAL? IS THIS REAL LIFE? MAYBE THE STORE MADE A MISTAKE. NO, MY FRIEND. YOU TAKE THAT DEAL AND YOU RUN, RUN AS FAST AS YOU CAN.

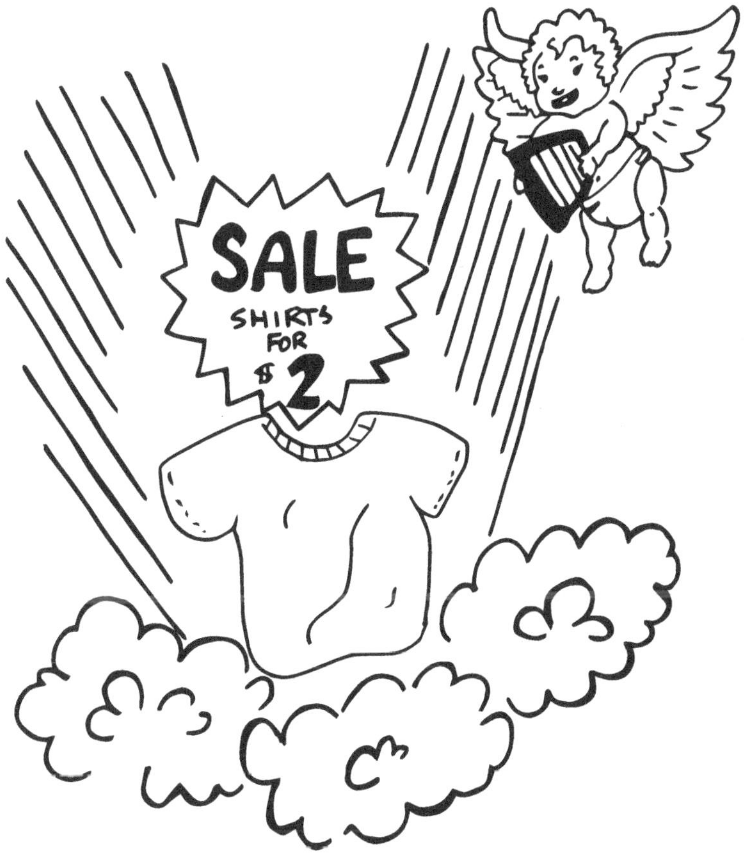
SALE
SHIRTS
FOR
$2

POPPING TAGS & CLIPPING COUPONS

GIFT-GIVING SEASON MAKES YOU S.WEAT

NOTHING LIKE THE HOLIDAYS TO MAKE YOUR WALLET WISH YOU DIDN'T HAVE ANY FRIENDS. WHILE SOME PEOPLE ARE SPREADING THE CHEER AROUND, YOU'RE MOURNING FOR YOUR BANK ACCOUNT AS YOU TRY TO AFFORD PRESENTS FROM THE DOLLAR STORE. IF YOU HAVE NO SHAME, YOU'LL PICK UP ANY RANDOM PIECE OF JUNK FROM A FLEA MARKET TO GIVE TO A FRIEND OR RE-GIFT THAT CHICKEN COOKIE JAR TO YOUR GRANDMOTHER, ONLY TO HAVE HER TELL YOU SHE GAVE IT TO YOU LAST YEAR. UH... SORRY, GRANDMA.

YOU HAVE PTSD FROM YOUR BLACK FRIDAY EXPEDITIONS.

It was the fall of 2004, 5am. There was a sale on big screen televisions and suburban mothers were readily equipped with shopping carts to slam into your back. You couldn't be scared—there was no time—as you dove headfirst into the crowd for discounted cameras and MP3 players. You almost lost an arm to the great videogame sales bin explosion. But you did it, kid. You got the sales.

Every Thanksgiving triggers those frightful memories of Black Friday mornings, and now that the madness begins after the turkey dinner, it just gets worse and worse. How many battle wounds do you have, the scars to remind you of the year of Tickle-Me-Elmo? You wonder if you should go back to the sales war, but you know inevitably it is your destiny. Brave on, soldier.

POPPING TAGS & CLIPPING COUPONS

NONE OF YOUR DESIGNER BRAND ITEMS ARE REAL, LET'S BE HONEST.

Louie Vutton
Fucci L'Boutin
Chanell Deor
Coache

OR THEY WERE BOUGHT FROM AN OUTLET STORE IN THE CLEARANCE RACK, LIKE THREE SEASONS BEHIND.

BUT YOU KNOW THE TRUTH. IT INVOLVED SOME SKETCH GUY IN AN ALLEY WITH AN OPENED CAR TRUNK—WHETHER HE OWNED THE CAR IS UNKNOWN—HOLDING UP "LOUIE VUTTON" AND "PUCCI" BAGS IN ONE HAND AND POSSIBLY STOLEN AIR JORDAN KICKS IN ANOTHER. YOU DIDN'T ASK QUESTIONS; YOU DIDN'T HAVE TO KNOW. IT WAS JUST A STRAIGHT BUSINESS TRANSACTION, THAT'S ALL. YEAH.

IF YOU BOUGHT IT, YOU'RE WEARING IT UNTIL IT DISINTEGRATES.

YOU'LL FIND ANOTHER REASON TO WEAR THAT WEDDING DRESS/TUX. NO NEED TO BUY ANY FORMAL ATTIRE WHEN YOU'RE CLEARLY ALREADY SET. WHY, IS IT A NICE SUMMER'S DAY TO PARADE AROUND IN YOUR WEDDING OUTFIT? OF COURSE IT IS. YOU DIDN'T SPEND HUNDREDS OF DOLLARS JUST TO WEAR THE THING ONCE, OKAY?

YOU'VE GOT PIECES OF CLOTHING IN YOUR CLOSET THAT ARE LITERALLY ON THEIR LAST THREADS. JEANS WITH HOLES, SHIRTS WITH HOLES, SHOES WITH HOLES—EVERYTHING WITH HOLES. IT'S NOT TIME TO GET RID OF CLOTHES UNTIL THEY FALL RIGHT OFF YOU. BUT, UH, MAKE SURE YOU DON'T END UP ACCIDENTALLY STREAKING IN PUBLIC.

EAT, PRAY, STARVE

THE FACT THAT YOU HAVE TO SPEND MONEY ON FOOD IN ORDER TO LIVE SEEMS LIKE BACKWARDS LOGIC, BUT UNLESS YOU'RE ABOUT TO BECOME A FARMER, SUCH IS THE WAY OF THE WORLD, MY FRIEND. YOUR FOOD PALETTE TAKES ON AN ENTIRELY DIFFERENT SPECTRUM THAN THAT OF YOUR ONE-PERCENTER COUNTERPART, WHOSE BOUGIE FOOD TASTES SPAN SIX OUT OF SEVEN CONTINENTS, WITH FOODS AND SPICES YOU'VE NEVER EVEN HEARD OF.

BUT YOU'RE A FOODIE OF SORTS, THE KIND OF FOODIE THAT CREATES RECIPES OUT OF THE THREE INGREDIENTS IN YOUR KITCHEN BECAUSE IT'S ALL YOU HAVE. YOU'VE CREATED CONCOCTIONS NO ONE IN THEIR RIGHT MIND WOULD PUT TOGETHER, AND YOU'VE EATEN ENOUGH SALT FROM INSTANT FOODS THAT PROBABLY WARRANT A TRIP TO THE EMERGENCY ROOM AT THE LEVELS YOUR BLOOD PRESSURE ARE HEADING. BUT WHAT DOESN'T KILL YOU ONLY MAKES YOUR STOMACH STRONGER, RIGHT?

EAT, PRAY, STARVE

THE ONLY PEOPLE WHO'VE EVER COOKED YOU FOOD WERE YOUR PARENTS.

YOU DON'T HAVE A SWEDISH CHEF TO COOK YOU A SMORGASBORD OF FOOD AND THE ONLY CUSTOM ORDERED MEALS YOU'RE GOING TO GET ARE SMILEY-FACED PANCAKES FROM YOUR MOM. UNLESS YOU PARTAKE IN THE CULINARY ARTS, CHANCES ARE THE MOMENT YOU HAD TO START COOKING FOR YOURSELF MEANT AN IMMEDIATE DECREASE IN THE QUALITY OF FOOD.

JUST TO AVOID COOKING, YOU HAVE TAKEN TO THE LEFT-OVER LIFESTYLE, THE MAKE-WHATEVER-YOU-HAVE RECIPES, THE EATING-CEREAL-FOR-DINNER ADULT DECISIONS. WHEN YOU'RE YOUR OWN CHEF, EATING ISN'T THAT SERIOUS. AIN'T NOBODY GOT TIME OR MONEY FOR ACTUAL FOOD (ESPECIALLY IN COLLEGE), LET ALONE COOKING MEALS LIKE A WELL-ADJUSTED INDIVIDUAL. IT'S NOT LIKE YOU REALLY NEED TO LIVE.

EAT, PRAY, STARVE

FREE FOOD IS YOUR MAIN *OBJECTIVE IN LIFE*.

CHANCES ARE, IF THERE'S FREE FOOD, YOU'RE HAVING IT. YOU DON'T EVEN REALLY CARE WHAT KIND OF FOOD, JUST AS LONG AS IT HAS THE WONDERFUL TASTE OF FREE.

WHETHER IT'S FREE SAMPLES AT THE MALL FOOD COURT OR COMPLIMENTARY BREAKFAST AT THE MOTEL YOU'RE STAYING AT, YOU TAKE EVERY OPPORTUNITY TO NOT BUY YOUR OWN FOOD. YOU MIGHT EVEN CALL IT YOUR MISSION IN LIFE. WHAT WOULD YOU DO FOR FREE FOOD? YOU DON'T KNOW. MAYBE KILL SOMEONE. YOU DON'T KNOW.

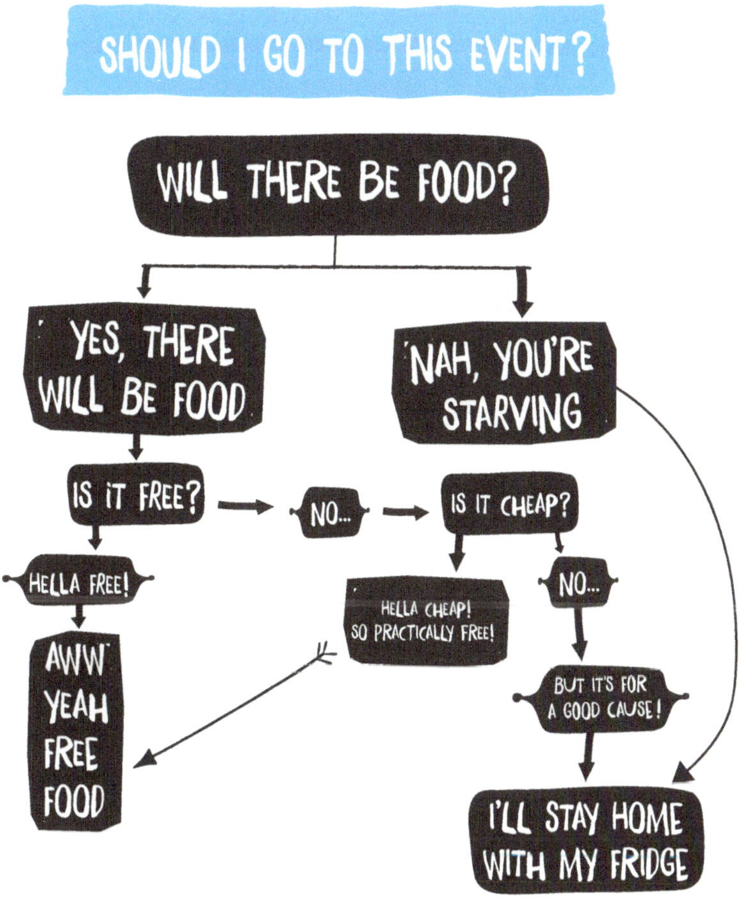
SHOULD I GO TO THIS EVENT?
WILL THERE BE FOOD?
YES, THERE WILL BE FOOD
NAH, YOU'RE STARVING
IS IT FREE?
NO...
IS IT CHEAP?
HELLA FREE!
HELLA CHEAP! SO PRACTICALLY FREE!
NO...
AWW YEAH FREE FOOD
BUT IT'S FOR A GOOD CAUSE!
I'LL STAY HOME WITH MY FRIDGE

EAT, PRAY, STARVE

YOU'VE GOT TAKE-OUT NUMBERS ON SPEED-DIAL. THEY KNOW YOUR ORDER. THEY KNOW YOUR NAME.

AT THIS POINT, YOU SHOULD SEND THE CHINESE RESTAURANT AROUND THE CORNER A "THANK YOU FOR BEING THERE" CARD. THEY'VE FED YOU SO OFTEN, THEY'RE PRACTICALLY FAMILY. AND THEY DON'T JUDGE YOU IF YOU ORDER THE FAMILY COMBO MEAL WHEN IT'S JUST YOU AT THE APARTMENT.

YOU HAVE AN ESTRANGED RELATIONSHIP WITH YOUR DELIVERY FOOD GUY. MAYBE YOU KNOW HIS NAME, MAYBE YOU DON'T. MAYBE YOU'RE BUILDING UP TO FINALLY HAVING A FULL-BLOWN

CONVERSATION WITH THE GUY. MAYBE YOU'LL INVITE HIM IN TO EAT WITH YOU, ESTABLISH A BEAUTIFUL FRIENDSHIP, TRAVEL THE WORLD TOGETHER, GROW OLD TOGETHER—AND AT HIS FUNERAL, YOU'LL FINALLY PAY THAT TWO-DOLLAR MINIMUM TIP.

REASONS WHY
Delivery Guy is your
SOULMATE

① HE BRINGS YOU FOOD

② NEVER JUDGES YOU ♥

③ GIVES YOU WHAT YOU WANT WHEN YOU WANT IT ～

④ **HE BRINGS YOU FOOD.**

EAT, PRAY, STARVE

TOP RAMEN IS ONE OF YOUR MAIN FOOD GROUPS. TOP RAMEN IS LIFE. TOP RAMEN IS FOREVER.

If there were a Top Ramen Anonymous group, you'd probably be in it for the amounts you've consumed in your life. No, seriously, you probably have high blood pressure from all that sodium intake. Go see a doctor, man.

But who could blame you? It's dirt cheap and lasts forever. It could probably even endure a nuclear holocaust. When the Japanese decided to make indestructible noodles, you figured that was a good step in the right direction. In the future, all food will be invincible, and ramen will come out on top.

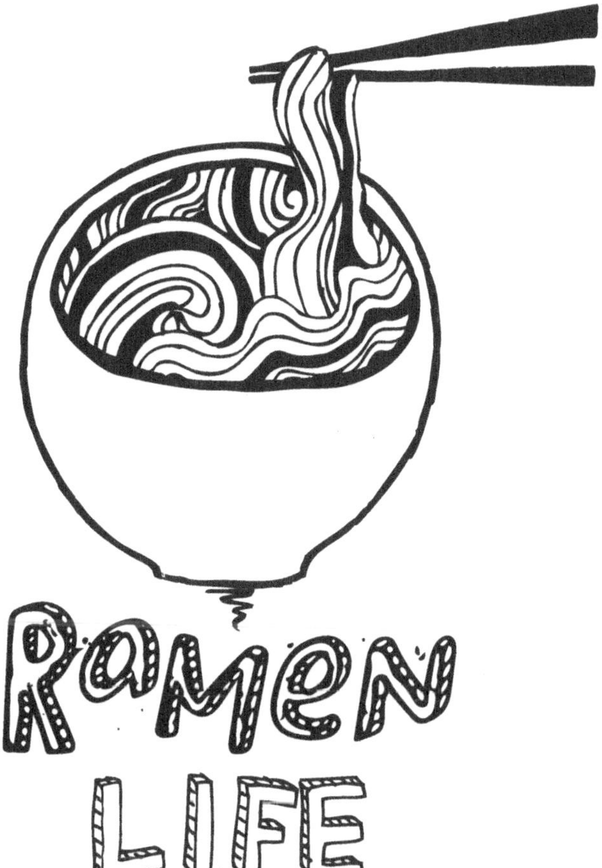
Ramen
LIFE

EAT, PRAY, STARVE

YOU TAKE FOOD *EXPIRATION DATES* AS A *CHALLENGE.*

PEOPLE IN THE UNITED STATES WASTE ABOUT A THIRD OF THEIR FOOD BECAUSE OF THEIR EXPIRATION, BUT NOT YOU, MY FRIEND. YOU AIN'T WASTING NOTHING. YOU BOUGHT THAT FOOD; YOU'RE GOING TO EAT THAT FOOD. WHEN YOU SEE MILK IN YOUR FRIDGE PAST ITS EXPIRATION DATE, FEAR DOES NOT STRIKE YOU.

EXPIRATION DATES ARE BUT MERE GUIDELINES THAT NEED TO BE BROKEN. CONSIDER YOURSELF LIVING LIFE ON THE EDGE, RISKING FOOD POISONING AT EVERY CORNER. YOU'VE DEVELOPED AN IRON STOMACH TO BE PROUD OF. THIS IS HOW YOU WEED OUT THE WEAK. NOW PASS THE SALT.

IRON STOMACH

ARE YOU NOT ENTERTAINED?

WATCH IT BATTLE:

- spoiled milk!
- moldy cheese
- undercooked chicken
- worm-infested apples!
- PURE ACID!!

IT CAN DEFEAT THEM ALL!

BEST BEFORE THE END OF THE WEEK

EXPIRED

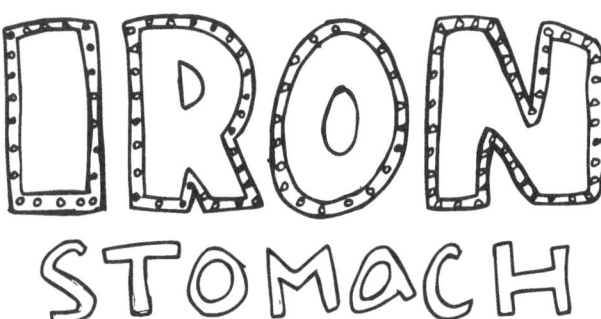

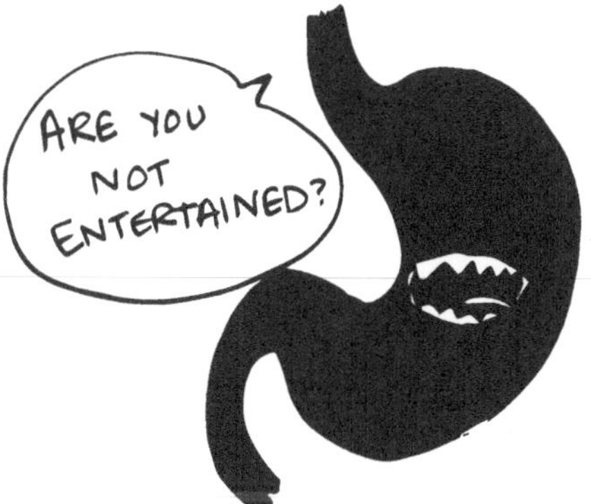

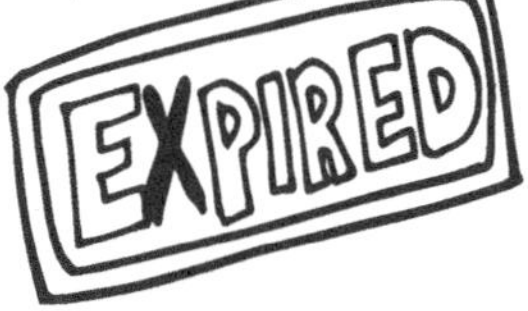

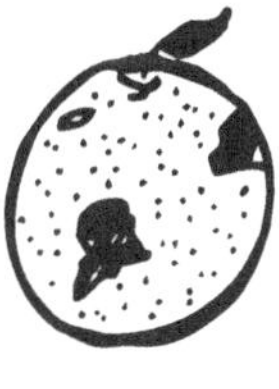

EAT, PRAY, STARVE

DROPPING MONEY ON RICH, COLOMBIAN COFFEE BEANS IS PRETTY MUCH LIKE YOU TRYING TO BUY RICH, COLOMBIAN COCAINE.

JUST GETTING STARBUCKS IS A TREAT, MAN.

THE PRICES ON COFFEE MAKES YOU WONDER IF DRINKING IT IS REALLY WORTH IT—AND EVERY TIME YOU FEEL THE ZING OF CAFFEINE SHOOT THROUGH YOUR VEINS AFTER DRINKING YOUR FIRST CUP OF JOE, YOU REALIZE, YES, YES IT IS. HOW COULD YOU HAVE EVER QUESTIONED IT? AH, LIKE A TRUE ADDICT, YOU'LL SETTLE FOR CHEAP INSTANT COFFEE JUST TO GET YOUR FIX THROUGHOUT THE WEEK, AND SPLURGE EVERY ONCE IN A WHILE ON A MOCHA LATTE, KNOWING THIS IS A HABIT YOU'LL NEVER KICK. THEY TRIED TO MAKE YOU GO TO REHAB, BUT YOU SAID NO, NO, NO.

BOXED WINE IS YOUR TYPICAL RED.

AIN'T NOTHING WRONG WITH A BOX OF FRANZIA IN YOUR PANTRY. WHILE OTHERS CAN HAVE THEIR FANCY MERLOTS AND CHARDONNAYS IN ACTUAL WINE BOTTLES, YOU PLAY IT ECONOMICALLY SAVVY WITH BAGGED WINE IN A CARDBOARD BOX. SOME PEOPLE MAY HAVE LABELED YOU AS A WINO, ACCUSING YOU OF CARING MORE ABOUT QUANTITY THAN QUALITY, BUT THEY'VE NEVER TASTED THE MAGIC THAT CAN BE CHEAP WINE, OKAY? FORGET THEM, MAN. JUST MORE WINE FOR YOU.

EAT, PRAY, STARVE

THE ORGANIC FOOD SECTION IN THE GROCERY STORE IS A WORLD UNKNOWN. 🍎

BUT SERIOUSLY, FOUR DOLLARS FOR AN APPLE?! HOW AMAZING DOES IT HAVE TO BE TO WARRANT THAT? IT DOESN'T MATTER HOW GREEN THE VEGETABLES LOOK OR HOW SWEET THE FRUIT MIGHT BE, UNTIL THE ORGANIC FOOD SECTION CAN JUSTIFY THE HIGHWAY ROBBERY IT'S TRYING TO PULL WITH THE PRICES THEY CHARGE, YOU'LL NEVER VENTURE INTO THAT SECTION OF THE GROCERY STORE.

AND LATELY, IT SEEMS EVERYTHING CAN BE ORGANIC. ORGANIC FRUITS AND VEGGIES, ORGANIC CHEESE, ORGANIC BREAD, ORGANIC WATER, ORGANIC ORGANS.

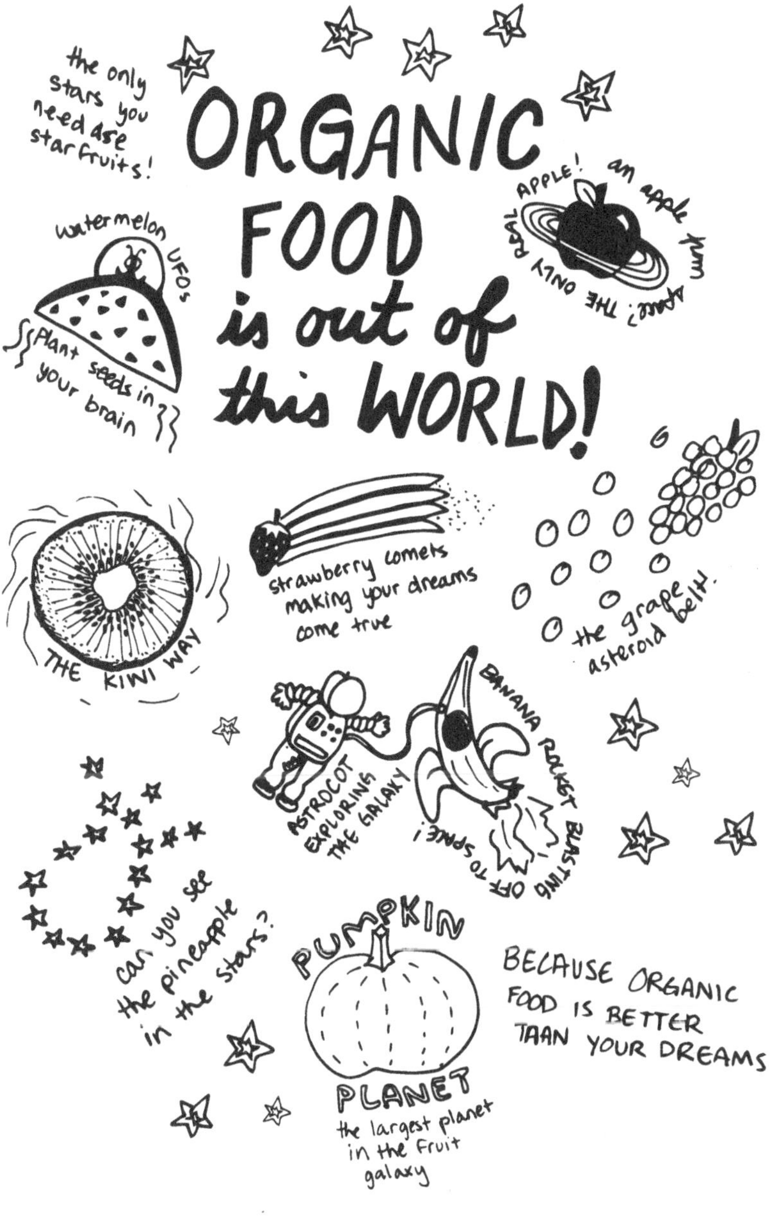
the only stars you need are starfruits!
ORGANIC FOOD is out of this WORLD!
an apple from space? THE ONLY REAL APPLE!
watermelon UFOs
Plant seeds in your brain
strawberry comets making your dreams come true
the grape asteroid belt!
THE KIWI WAY
ASTROCOT EXPLORING THE GALAXY
BANANA ROCKET BLASTING OFF TO SPACE!
can you see the pineapple in the stars?
PUMPKIN PLANET
the largest planet in the Fruit galaxy
BECAUSE ORGANIC FOOD IS BETTER THAN YOUR DREAMS

EAT, PRAY, STARVE

BUFFETS ARE THE WATERING HOLES OF LIFE.

AH, ALL-YOU-CAN-EAT BUFFETS. TRULY, A SPECTACLE OF THE MASSES. YOU COULD EASILY WIN A BINGO GAME BASED AROUND PEOPLE'S BUFFET OUTFITS, MARKING OFF ALL THE MOM AND DAD JEANS, THE CHEETAH SPANDEX LEGGINGS, THE WASHED-OUT PATRIOTIC EAGLE T-SHIRTS (BONUS POINTS IF THEY'RE SLEEVELESS). IT'S A FASHION TABOO WONDERLAND. A DINNER AND A SHOW.

AS FOR THE FOOD, IT DEPENDS ON YOUR MOOD, BUT ABSOLUTELY EVERYTHING IS BOUND TO CLOG YOUR ARTERIES. THIS IS WHERE CREATIVITY IS BORN, AS YOU STACK SOUTHERN-STYLE MAC AND CHEESE ONTO YOUR BURGER AND DIP SWEET POTATOES INTO YOUR CHILI. IT IS A CARB FEST, A GREASE EXTRAVAGANZA, A CARNIVAL OF SWEETS—AND WHEN YOU'RE DONE, YOU'LL DIE HAPPY.

YOU CONSIDER THE LOCAL, ITALIAN FAMILY-STYLE RESTAURANT "FINE-DINING."

NEVER-ENDING SOUP AND SALAD WOULD SEEM LIKE A LUXURY, WHAT WITH HAVING INFINITE AMOUNTS OF FOOD AT YOUR DISPOSAL, BUT IT'S THE PLASTIC BABY HIGH CHAIRS THAT KEEP YOU GROUNDED, AS YOU TRY TO EAT SIX OVERPRICED JUMBO SHRIMP TO THE TUNES OF BICKERING COUPLES AND WHINING CHILDREN IN THEIR RESPECTIVE BOOTHS.

IF THERE'S A SENIOR MENU FOR THE ELDERLY AND TWO-FOR-ONE DEALS FOR COLLEGE COUPLES TRYING TO AFFORD A GOOD TIME, THEN YOUR RUN-OF-THE-MILL BLUE COLLAR EATERY IS NOT A PLACE YOU'LL FIND SOMEONE WEARING A ROLEX AS THEY HAND OVER THEIR AMERICAN EXPRESS CREDIT CARD.

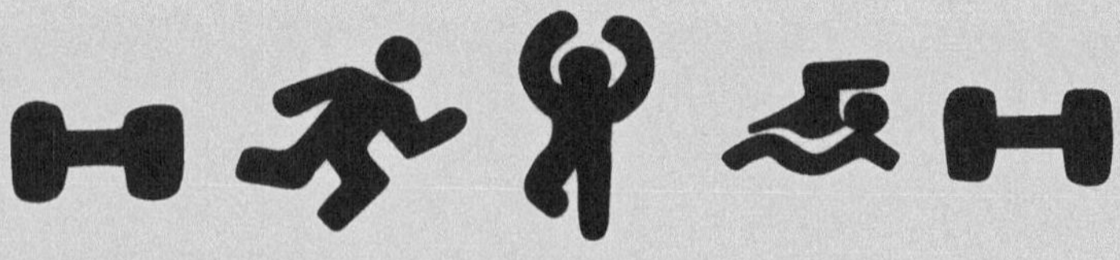

LOSE WEIGHT LIKE YOU LOSE MONEY

IF YOU LOST A POUND FOR EVERY DOLLAR YOU LOST FROM YOUR WALLET, YOU'D PROBABLY CEASE TO EXIST. WHAT HAPPENED TO THE DAYS WHEN THE RICH WERE NOTORIOUS FOR BEING FAT? NOW THEY'RE HEALTHY AND SKINNY, TOO?

YOUR MEANS OF TRYING TO KEEP UP WITH THE LATEST TRENDS IN EXERCISE AND DIET STEMS FROM ANYTHING THAT'S FREE FOR EVERYONE, WHETHER YOU'RE GETTING YOUR AEROBICS ROUTINE FROM AN APP YOU DOWNLOADED OFF YOUR PHONE OR WATCHING DR. OZ ON PBS TO REMEMBER IF EGGS WERE GOOD FOR YOU OR NOT. BUT NO MATTER WHAT, JUST TRYING TO KEEP HEALTHY IS AN ORDEAL.

LOSE WEIGHT LIKE YOU LOSE MONEY

YOU'LL BE DAMNED IF YOU GO TO THE DOCTOR BEFORE YOU ABSOLUTELY HAVE TO. LIKE, YOUR LEG GOT CHOPPED OFF. AND EVEN THEN, MAYBE.

FOR WHAT IT COSTS TO GO TO THE DOCTOR, IT IS ABSOLUTELY THE LAST RESORT FOR YOU. WEIRD RASH ON YOUR ARM? WINDEX IT. ODD MOLE ON YOUR BACK? EH, WAIT TWO YEARS AND SEE IF IT GROWS. PROBABLY ISN'T SERIOUS CANCER. SOME DEEPLY CONCERNING INFECTION CREEPING UP YOUR LEG? IT'LL PASS...

TO GET THROUGH LIFE, YOU NEED A HIGH PAIN INTOLERANCE, AND YOUR IMMUNITY SYSTEM IS NO BETA CHUMP TO DISEASE. WHAT'S NECESSARY ABOUT A "CHECK-UP" ANYWAY? IF YOU DON'T FEEL WRONG, THEN EVERYTHING'S FINE, RIGHT? IT'S OKAY TO SPIT OUT BLOOD SOMETIMES, RIGHT?

NEED AN EXPENSIVE SURGERY?
SUCKS FOR YOU.

WHAT IS HEALTH INSURANCE ANYWAY? SEEMS LIKE A NEAT IDEA. YOU MEAN THERE ARE PEOPLE WHO CAN AFFORD TO FIX THEIR HIPS AND BACKS AND STUFF? LIKE THEY DON'T HAVE TO LIVE IN AGONIZING PAIN EVERY WAKING MOMENT? THEY CAN BE HEALTHY HUMAN BEINGS? WHAT A TIME TO BE ALIVE.

YOU'LL JUST STAY AT HOME, HACKING YOUR LUNGS OUT. IF ONE OF THEM REALLY COMES OUT, MAYBE YOU COULD SELL IT ON THE BLACK MARKET. IT MIGHT COVER THE HOSPITAL BILLS.

LOSE WEIGHT LIKE YOU LOSE MONEY

YOU DO YOGA IN YOUR LIVING ROOM, NOT ON A MOUNTAIN CLIFF AT DAWN.

WHEN YOU DO "DOWNWARDS DOG," YOU INHALE THE SWEET SCENTS OF STAINED CARPET AND A SWEAT-RIDDEN YOGA MAT, NOT FRESH AIR FROM THE VALLEY. YOU MEDITATE TO THE SOUNDS OF LAWN MOWERS CUTTING THE GRASS AND TRAFFIC JAM HONKS AND BEEPS. IT MIGHT BE TOLERABLE WHEN YOU LIVE ALONE, BUT ACHIEVING NIRVANA IS ESPECIALLY DIFFICULT WHEN CURIOUS DOGS AND CHILDREN SPIN AROUND YOUR LEGS, MAKING YOUR UPRIGHT TREE COME CRASHING DOWN.

YOUR INNER YOGI WOULD LOVE TO HAVE YOUR ROOFTOP GAZE OUT INTO A MOUNTAINSIDE LANDSCAPE, BUT NO. ENJOY THE SERENITY OF BRICK WALLS AND NEIGHBORS IN THEIR UNDERWEAR, WONDERING WHAT YOU'RE DOING.

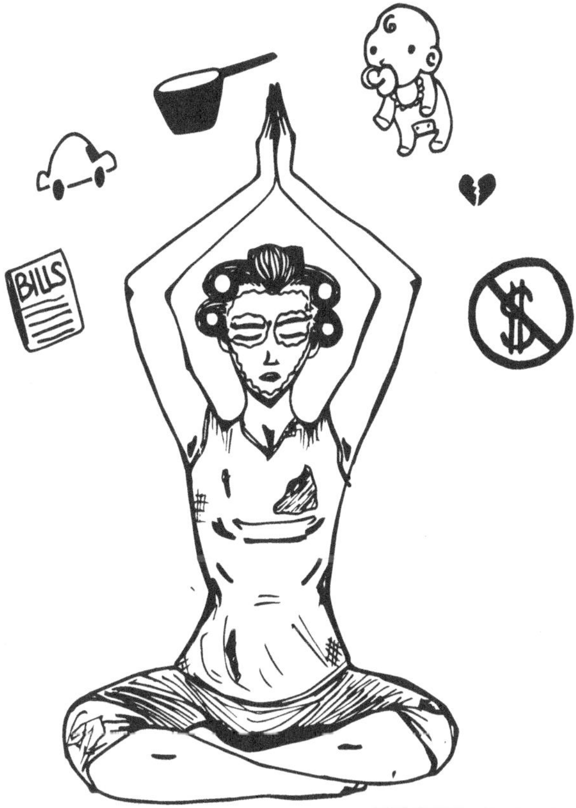
BILLS

LOSE WEIGHT LIKE YOU LOSE MONEY

YOU ONLY TAKE YOGA/PILATES CLASSES THROUGH GROUPON DEALS.

THE FACT THAT YOU'VE NEVER CONTINUED ANY OF THOSE CLASSES WITH THE SAME INSTRUCTOR IS JUST YOU TRYING TO KEEP IT FRESH. SPICING IT UP EVERY TEN WEEKS HAS NOTHING TO DO WITH THE FACT THAT THE GROUPON DEAL EXPIRED AND NOW THEY'RE ASKING FOR A MEMBERSHIP FEE—BUT LIKE, HOW DARE THEY? YOU'RE A FREE SPIRIT WHO CAN'T BE TIED DOWN TO CONTRACTUAL GYM MEMBERSHIPS, YOU KNOW?

HONESTLY.

YOUR PERSONAL GYM CONSISTS OF A BUSTED UP STATIONARY BIKE, YOUTUBE VIDEOS, AND A DREAM.

FORGET FANCY EQUIPMENT AND PERSONAL TRAINERS, LIKE THE ONE-PERCENTERS USE. YOU'RE CREATIVE; YOU'RE RESOURCEFUL. NOW WITH ALL SORTS OF YOUTUBE VIDEOS BOOTLEGGING EXERCISE COURSES ONLINE, WHY EVEN BOTHER GOING TO THE GYM WHEN YOU CAN LEARN GYPSY DANCING AT A SIDE CAMERA ANGLE? SURE, THE MUSIC CAN BARELY BE HEARD OVER THE NOISE VOLUME AND SNEAKERS SQUEAKING FROM THE PEOPLE ACTUALLY PAYING FOR THE COURSE, BUT WHATEVER. YOU'LL DEAL.

THERE ARE ALL SORTS OF APPS TO MONITOR YOUR EATING HABITS LIKE ANY QUALIFIED NUTRITIONIST, AND SOME EVEN INSTRUCT YOU HOW TO DO WEIGHTS LIKE A PERSONAL TRAINER! WELL, TO A POINT. THEY CAN'T NECESSARILY READJUST YOUR ARM A FRACTION OF AN INCH TO PREVENT YOU FROM PULLING A MUSCLE LIKE AN INSTRUCTOR COULD DO IN PERSON, BUT THOSE ARE JUST DETAILS.

LOSE WEIGHT LIKE YOU LOSE MONEY

TRYING TO SPOT HOTTIES AT THE "Y" IS ROUGH.

IF YOU COULD AFFORD A PROPER GYM MEMBERSHIP AT A CELEBRITY-ENDORSED L.A. GYM, MAYBE YOU'D HAVE MORE LUCK SPOTTING A WORKOUT CUTIE TO CHECK OUT, BUT INSTEAD YOU'VE GOT THE RANDOM SELECTS AT THE YMCA. OCCASIONALLY YOU MIGHT FIND THAT CUTE YOUNG STUDENT RUNNING ON THE TREADMILL—UNTIL YOU LEARN THEY'RE A HIGH SCHOOL STUDENT, AND NOW THEY'RE NOT CUTE AT ALL—WHAT? YOU NEVER SAID THAT. OH GOD. BACK AWAY. MAKE NO EYE CONTACT. CANCEL YOUR MEMBERSHIP. RUN.

SHOULD I GO TO THE GYM?

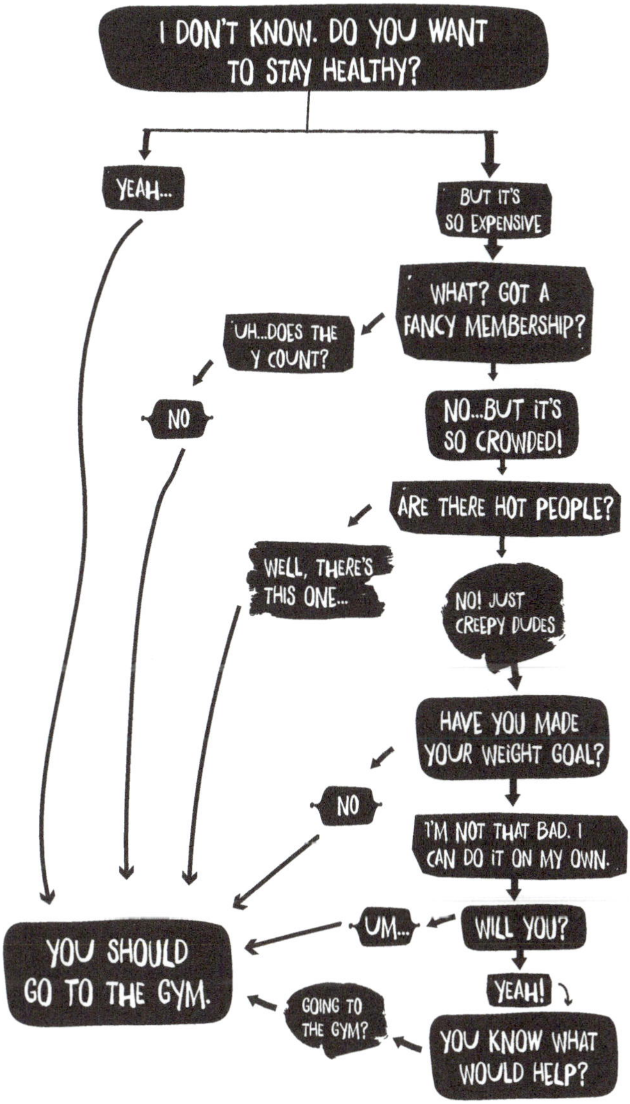
I DON'T KNOW. DO YOU WANT TO STAY HEALTHY?
YEAH...
BUT IT'S SO EXPENSIVE
WHAT? GOT A FANCY MEMBERSHIP?
UH...DOES THE Y COUNT?
NO
NO...BUT IT'S SO CROWDED!
ARE THERE HOT PEOPLE?
WELL, THERE'S THIS ONE...
NO! JUST CREEPY DUDES
HAVE YOU MADE YOUR WEIGHT GOAL?
NO
I'M NOT THAT BAD. I CAN DO IT ON MY OWN.
WILL YOU?
UM...
YEAH!
YOU KNOW WHAT WOULD HELP?
GOING TO THE GYM?
YOU SHOULD GO TO THE GYM.

LOSE WEIGHT LIKE YOU LOSE MONEY

==While some learned the art of ballet or the tango, you learned the fine practice of booty dancing== and doing the cha-cha slide now, y'all.

You may not know the proper steps to waltz around a ballroom, but you can whip out some sick moves on the dancefloor. Whether you're the pop and lock-ness monster with the smoothest robot wave to make every B-boy proud or pulling out the ol' Macarena to get jiggy with it, your motion expression will awe the lands. You don't need structured steps to feel the music, man.

The one-percent may have their classy, award-winning dances, but one time you won a dance-a-thon for doing the chicken dance for twelve whole hours and won a year-supply of fried chicken from the local grocery store, so like, who's the winner now?

Mythical Dancing MONSTERS

THE POP-AND-LOCK NESS MONSTER

← killing it in the Scottish Highlands!

BIG "TWO-LEFT" FOOT

← can't dance, but he tries

VOGUEZILLA

← so couture in Tokyo!

THE GO-GO GHOST

← haunting you with her groovy moves

THE ELECTRIC SLIDE-CLOPS

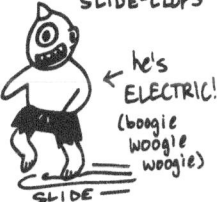

← he's ELECTRIC! (boogie woogie woogie)

— SLIDE —

WHIP-MY-TAIL WEREWOLF

← he whips his tail back and forth; he whips it REAL HARD

THE LIMBO TROLL

← how low can you go?

← he won't let you pass until you do the limbo

GANGNAMSTEIN'S MONSTER

— UHHHH SEXY LADY UGH UGH UGH UGUH

Lose weight like you lose money

IN WALK-A-THON DONATIONS, YOU DO MAYBE $25 PER MILE
... AND YOU WALK ONLY A MILE.

Okay, this one makes you sound bad, but honestly, it's hard being charitable when you need the charity. No one told you the monetary amount you put down for donation was per mile you walked, so you might have accidentally started sobbing uncontrollably at the finish line when they congratulated you for your ambitious $1000 donation for all those miles you walked! You're such a great person!

At this rate, you might want to try to organize a charity event in your name. You know, before you lose the house or something.

135

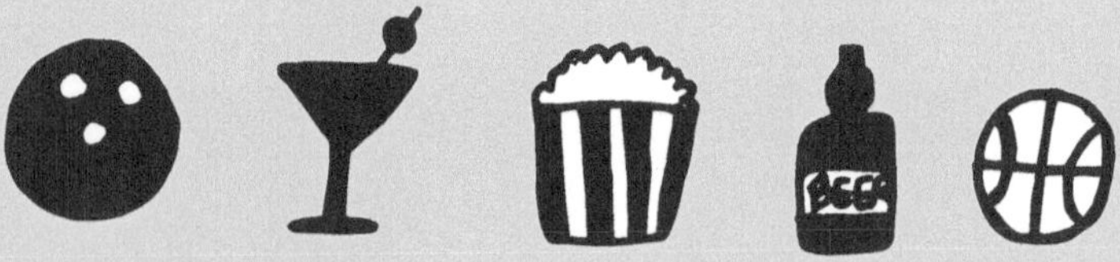
BEER

THE SACRED HOURS OF THE WEEKEND

THERE ARE TWO DAYS OF THE WEEK THAT ARE YOURS: SATURDAY AND SUNDAY. THEY ARE THE ONLY DAYS THAT REMIND YOU OF THE OUTSIDE WORLD, WHAT HAVING FRIENDS FEELS LIKE, AND WHAT HAPPENED IN LAST WEEK'S EPISODE OF YOUR FAVORITE DRAMA. YOU TAKE THESE DAYS VERY SERIOUSLY AND NO ONE, NO ONE, WILL TAKE THEM AWAY FROM YOU.

NOW IF ONLY YOU COULD FIGURE OUT WHAT TO DO ON THOSE DAYS...

THE SACRED HOURS OF THE WEEKEND

WORK HARD, PARTY REASONABLY PRICED, PREFERABLY ON A SATURDAY, NO LATER THAN 1AM —ACTUALLY CAN YOU STAY HOME?

IF YOU HAD THE KIND OF SALARY TO BLOW ON RITZY STUDIO 54-ESQUE NIGHTCLUBS ON LIKE A TUESDAY, THEN MAYBE YOU'D BE LESS OF A GRUMPY PANTS WHO NEEDS TO BE UP BY SIX IN THE MORNING THE NEXT DAY. BUT RESPONSIBILITIES, MAN. NOTHING IS WORSE THAN GOING TO WORK HUNG OVER. TRYING TO DO FIGURES WHILE YOUR BRAIN WANTS TO RIP ITSELF IN HALF? UH, NO THANK YOU.

AND ANY TIME YOU DO HAVE TO YOURSELF IN THE EVENING IS GOING STRAIGHT TO SLEEP. YOUR BED IS YOUR NIGHTCLUB. THE BLANKETS ARE THE BOUNCERS. AND YOU'LL BE GOING TO BED WITH A SWEET LOVER NAMED PILLOW.

SHOULD I GO OUT TONIGHT?

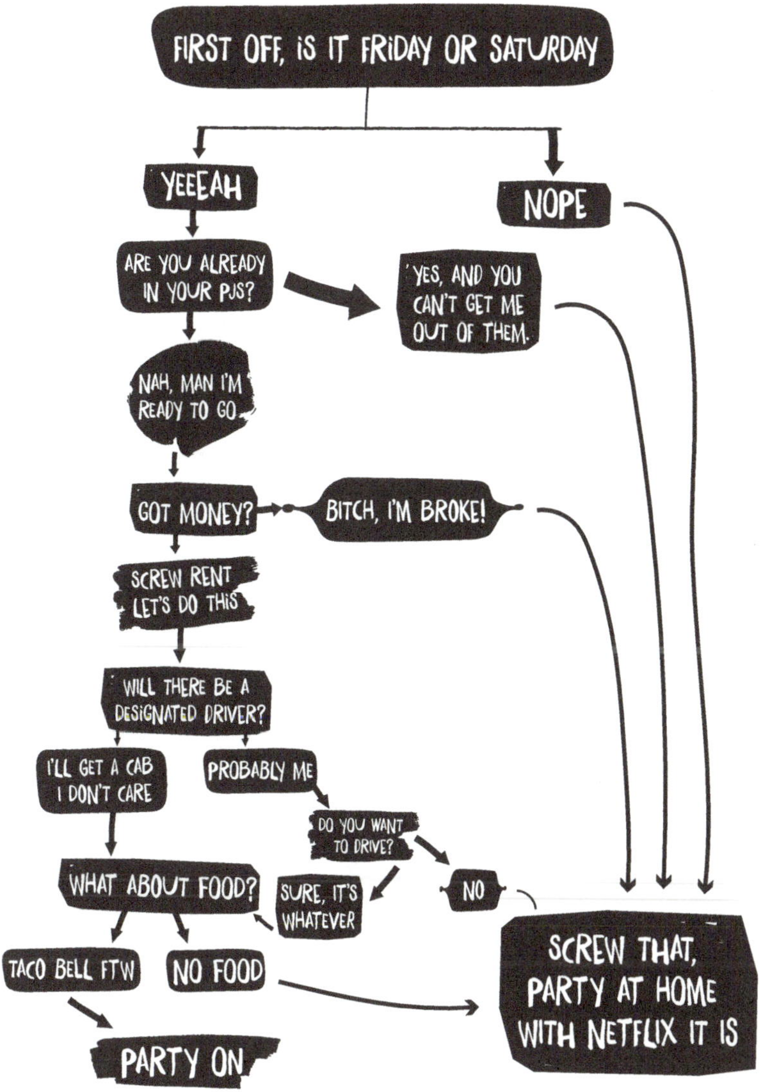
FIRST OFF, IS IT FRIDAY OR SATURDAY
YEEEAH
NOPE
ARE YOU ALREADY IN YOUR PJS?
YES, AND YOU CAN'T GET ME OUT OF THEM.
NAH, MAN I'M READY TO GO.
GOT MONEY?
BITCH, I'M BROKE!
SCREW RENT LET'S DO THIS
WILL THERE BE A DESIGNATED DRIVER?
I'LL GET A CAB I DON'T CARE
PROBABLY ME
DO YOU WANT TO DRIVE?
SURE, IT'S WHATEVER
NO
WHAT ABOUT FOOD?
TACO BELL FTW
NO FOOD
PARTY ON
SCREW THAT, PARTY AT HOME WITH NETFLIX IT IS

THE SACRED HOURS OF THE WEEKEND

YOU ONLY GO OUT WITH YOUR FRIENDS IF IT'S **FREE OR** MAD **CHEAP.**

FRIENDSHIP IS FREE AND SO SHOULD BE WHAT YOU GUYS DO TOGETHER. WHY MAKE FUN EXPENSIVE WHEN YOU CAN GO BOWLING ON DOLLAR-GAME MONDAYS, HIT THE ART MUSEUM ON OPEN HOUSE THURSDAYS, SING SOME KARAOKE CLASSICS AT THE SUSHI BUFFET ON OPEN MIC NIGHT, AND EAT NOTHING BUT 25-CENT CHICKEN WINGS ON FOOTBALL SUNDAYS? LIKE, YOU HAVE A SCHEDULE. SOMETIMES, IF YOU GUYS FEEL CRAZY AND WANT TO GO WILD, YOU'LL DONATE BLOOD FOR FREE MOVIE TICKETS AND DOUBLE FEATURE THAT SHIT.

NOSEBLEED SEATS AT THE STADIUM
MEANS ELEVATED SEATS FOR WATCHING TELEVISION.

WHY DO NOSEBLEED SEATS EVEN EXIST ANYWAY? YOU CAN BARELY SEE ANYTHING. AND YOU'D HAVE TO LOOK AT THE SCREEN UP AHEAD IN THE END JUST TO KNOW WHAT'S GOING ON, WHAT WITH THE BASKETBALL TEAM LOOKING LIKE A BUNCH OF AMOEBAS IN UNIFORM. IMAGINE WHAT IT WOULD BE LIKE TO WATCH THE SWEAT DRIP OFF LEBRON JAMES AS HE DODGES OPPONENTS ON THE BASKETBALL COURT, OR ACTUALLY HEAR BONES CRACK AS YOU WATCH FOOTBALL PLAYERS TACKLE EACH OTHER INTO THE GROUND.

ALL YOU WANT IS A CHANCE TO SEE FAMOUS PEOPLE THROW A BALL AROUND. IS IT SO MUCH TO ASK?

THE SACRED HOURS OF THE WEEKEND

YOU SMUGGLE IN SNACKS AND DRINKS INTO THE MOVIES TO SHARE WITH YOUR FRIENDS LIKE IT'S CONTRABAND.

YOU KNOW THE DEAL. WHOEVER HAS THE LARGEST PURSE/BAG IS THE DRUG MULE OF THE PACK, STORING DOLLAR STORE CANDY, SODA BOTTLES, BAG OF CHIPS, WHATEVER. HELL, IF YOU'RE FEELING BALLSY ENOUGH, YOU'LL BRING A FOOT-LONG SUB SANDWICH. WHO'S GOING TO STOP YOU?

YOU'VE FELT THE HIGH THAT COMES WITH STARING AN USHER DOWN AS YOU WALK INTO A THEATRE ROOM WITH ILLEGAL GUMMY BEARS SHOVED UNDER YOUR SHIRT AND NOW YOU'LL NEVER STOP. MAKES YOU FEEL ALIVE.

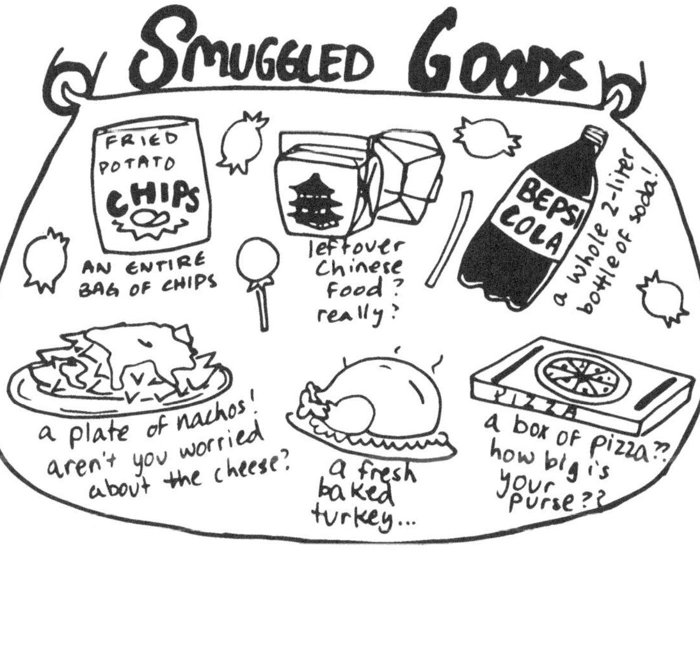
SMUGGLED GOODS
FRIED POTATO CHIPS
AN ENTIRE BAG OF CHIPS
leftover Chinese food? really?
BEPSI COLA
a whole 2-liter bottle of soda!
a plate of nachos! aren't you worried about the cheese?
a fresh baked turkey...
PIZZA
a box of pizza?? how big is your purse??

THE SACRED HOURS OF THE WEEKEND

==LEGITIMATELY CONSIDERED SMUGGLING ONE OF YOUR FRIENDS IN THE TRUNK IF IT MEANT SAVING MONEY.==

No joke, sometimes the situation calls for it. A night at the flea market drive-in theatre or a drive down a safari zoo path sounds nice until they try to charge per person instead of per car. That's when the tiniest one of your crew gets shoved in the trunk, because that's what friendship is all about: cheating the system together.

> **YOU WATCHED CHICAGO THE MUSICAL AT A HIGH SCHOOL PERFORMANCE, NOT ON BROADWAY.**

THE HIGH SCHOOL DRAMA CLUB WAS AWKWARDLY MEDIOCRE AT BEST, IF YOU HAD TO JUDGE IT, BUT THE CARDBOARD CITYSCAPE IN THE BACKGROUND WAS KIND OF COOL. STILL, IT'S NO BROADWAY MUSICAL WITH SPECIAL GUEST APPEARANCE, NEIL PATRICK HARRIS. YOUR NIGHT AT THE THEATRE INVOLVES LISTENING TO TEENAGERS WITH PITCHY VOCALS ATTEMPTING TO REMEMBER THEIR LINES, MAKING YOU CRINGE WHEN ONE OF THEM STARES INTO THE ABYSS THAT IS YOU—THEIR AUDIENCE—AND FREEZES.

HEY, IF THE HIGH SCHOOL PERFORMANCE WAS A HORROR PLAY, THEY WOULD HAVE NAILED THE FEAR DOWN, RIGHT?

BLACKBEARD WOULD BE IMPRESSED BY THE AMOUNT OF MEDIA YOU PIRATE ONLINE.

IT'S GOTTEN TO THE POINT THAT IF THE FBI EVER CATCHES YOU, YOU KNOW YOU'RE GOING TO JAIL.

YOUR REPERTOIRE OF ILLEGALLY DOWNLOADED MATERIALS RANGES ACROSS ALL MEDIA: FROM THE LATEST ALBUM DROPPED BY BEYONCÉ TO THE BLOCKBUSTER FILM COMING TO THEATRES NEXT WEEK (YOU HAVE NO SHAME, MY GOD). WHO NEEDS TO PAY FOR HBO WHEN YOU'VE GOT SKETCHY, POSSIBLY VIRUS-RIDDEN, RUSSIAN-BASED, LIVE-STREAMING WEBSITES TO GIVE YOU YOUR FIX OF THE LATEST EPISODES OF GAME OF THRONES? YOU DO WHAT YOU HAVE TO DO TO KEEP UP WITH THE TIMES.

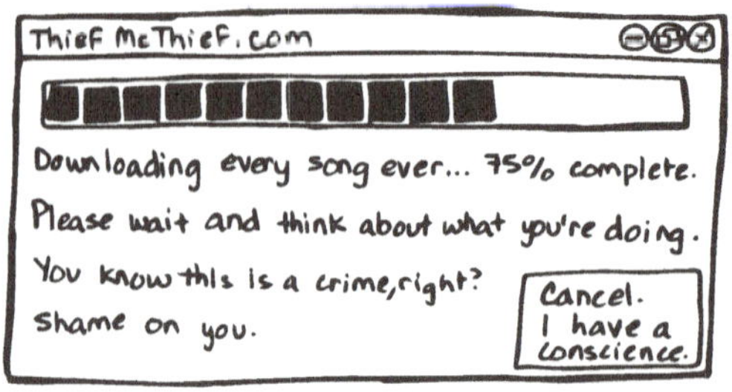
ThiefMcThief.com
Downloading every song ever... 75% complete.
Please wait and think about what you're doing.
You know this is a crime, right?
Shame on you.
Cancel.
I have a conscience.

You have a library card, but not a personal library.

You're pretty proud of your bookshelf, though, which you've spent hours upon hours reorganizing to showcase who you are. But at the end of the day, it's no Oxford room in the nook of your establishment, where all your leather-bound books reside.

But forget about appearing literary and cultured. If you are, you are, man. While the pretentious may rave on with an eighth-grade level analysis on The Great Gatsby, you can explore the public library, discovering great 99% authors, like Junot Diaz, Ray Bradbury, and Joan Didion.

THE SACRED HOURS OF THE WEEKEND

YEAH, YOU HAVE A SAILBOAT. IN THE BATHTUB.

YOU WANT TO START SAILING AWAY, BUDDY? THEN YOU MIGHT AS WELL SIT YOURSELF IN AN INNER TUBE, HOLD UP A BLANKET, AND HOPE FOR THE BEST, MAN. JUST DON'T GET EATEN BY SHARKS, OKAY?

YOU GET PISSED OFF WHEN A NEW AND BETTER TECHNOLOGICAL DEVICE COMES OUT... RIGHT AFTER YOU BOUGHT YOURS.

...TWO DAYS AGO.

COME ON! IS NOTHING SACRED? IT'S LIKE COMPANIES KNOW THE EXACT DAY YOU BOUGHT YOUR ITEM, JUST SO THEY COULD TANTALIZE YOU WITH A NEW ONE A FEW HOURS LATER. YOU CAN'T AFFORD TO KEEP UP WITH THE TRENDS, MAN. TECHNOLOGY ADVANCES TOO FAST FOR YOUR WALLET. YOU DIDN'T CHOOSE THE 99% LIFE, THE 99% LIFE CHOSE YOU.

LIKELIHOOD THAT NEW CELL PHONE WILL COME OUT...
ALWAYS
...AFTER YOU JUST BOUGHT YOURS

HOW YOU TAKE THE NEWS...
THINGS THAT ARE OKAY
• YOU
MAYBE NEXT YEAR, BUDDY.

THE SACRED HOURS OF THE WEEKEND

GETTING RETWEETED BY A CELEBRITY ON TWITTER IS ABOUT AS CLOSE AS YOU'LL GET TO THE RICH AND FAMOUS.

IT MIGHT HAVE MADE YOUR DAY, YOUR WEEK, YOUR LIFE.

NOW WITH SOCIAL MEDIA APPLICATIONS, IT'S EASIER THAN EVER TO BE GRACED UPON BY YOUR IDOLS, WHETHER IT'S A SMILEY FACE RETWEET ON TWITTER OR A COMMENT REPLY ON THEIR FACEBOOK PAGE. SURE, IT'S NOT THE SAME AS HAVING THE SOCIALITE LIFESTYLE, WHERE YOU HOLD BACK A FASHION MODEL'S HAIR AFTER A NIGHT OF PARTYING, BUT YOU'LL ALWAYS HAVE THAT TUMBLR REBLOG FROM MARK RUFFALO TO CHEER YOU UP AT NIGHT, KNOWING HE LIKED YOUR POST ABOUT CATS.

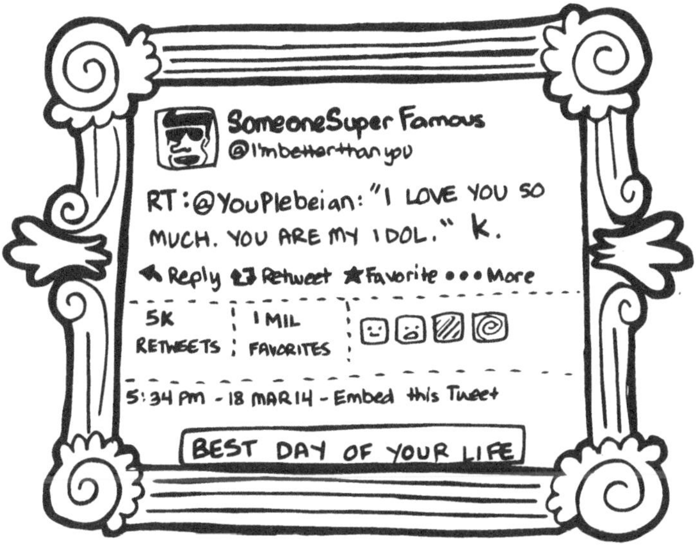
SomeoneSuper Famous
@I'mbetterthanyou
RT: @YouPlebeian: "I LOVE YOU SO MUCH. YOU ARE MY IDOL." K.
Reply Retweet Favorite More
5K RETWEETS
1 MIL FAVORITES
5:34 PM - 18 MAR 14 - Embed this Tweet
BEST DAY OF YOUR LIFE

THE BIG DAYS OF YOUR LITTLE LIFE

THERE ARE CERTAIN MILESTONES IN LIFE THAT EVERYONE GOES THROUGH, WHERE THE SPECIAL OCCASION GIVES WAY TO SPLURGING ON YOURSELF A BIT AND BRINGING OUT THE FINE CHINA. BUT ALL WITH DUE MEASURE, MY FRIEND, FOR YOU ARE STILL NOT PART OF THE TOP 1% AND CAN'T AFFORD TO BRING LIONS TO YOUR SWEET SIXTEEN AS YOUR DEBUT ENTOURAGE—WAIT, YOU HAVE AN ENTOURAGE?—NOR CAN YOU SCATTER CAVIAR AND CHAMPAGNE ALL OVER YOUR GUESTS AS YOU SHOWER THEM WITH MONEY AND GOLD.

BUT YOU CAN STILL HAVE ONE HELL OF A PARTY, EVEN WITHOUT ALL THAT.

the big days of your little life

YOU'RE NOT REALLY SURE WHAT A DEBUTANTE BALL IS. ONE TIME YOU WENT TO A BAR MITZVAH. DOES THAT COUNT?

LIKE, IT SORT OF DOES? BUT NO, MAN, THE AVERAGE BAR MITZVAH AT THE PIZZA PARLOR DOES NOT COUNT. IF THERE ARE PAPER STRIPS HANGING FROM THE CEILING INSTEAD OF A CRYSTAL DIAMOND GARLAND AND DJ OFF OF CRAIGSLIST PLAYING LAST YEAR'S TOP 40 HITS INSTEAD OF A LIVE BAND ROCKING THE STAGE, THEN YOU HAVE NEVER WITNESSED SOMEONE PRESENT THEMSELVES TO THE WORLD WITH A MILLION DOLLAR BANG.

BUT HEY, WHO NEEDS TO BE FANCY AT A SWEET SIXTEEN WHEN YOU CAN HAVE THE CRAZED ADVENTURES OF WATCHING YOUR COUSIN SPIKE THE FRUIT PUNCH WITH LIQUOR AND THEN SEEING YOUR UNCLE GET DRUNK ON THE DANCEFLOOR WITH A PLANT AS HIS DANCE PARTNER. STORY OF A LIFETIME.

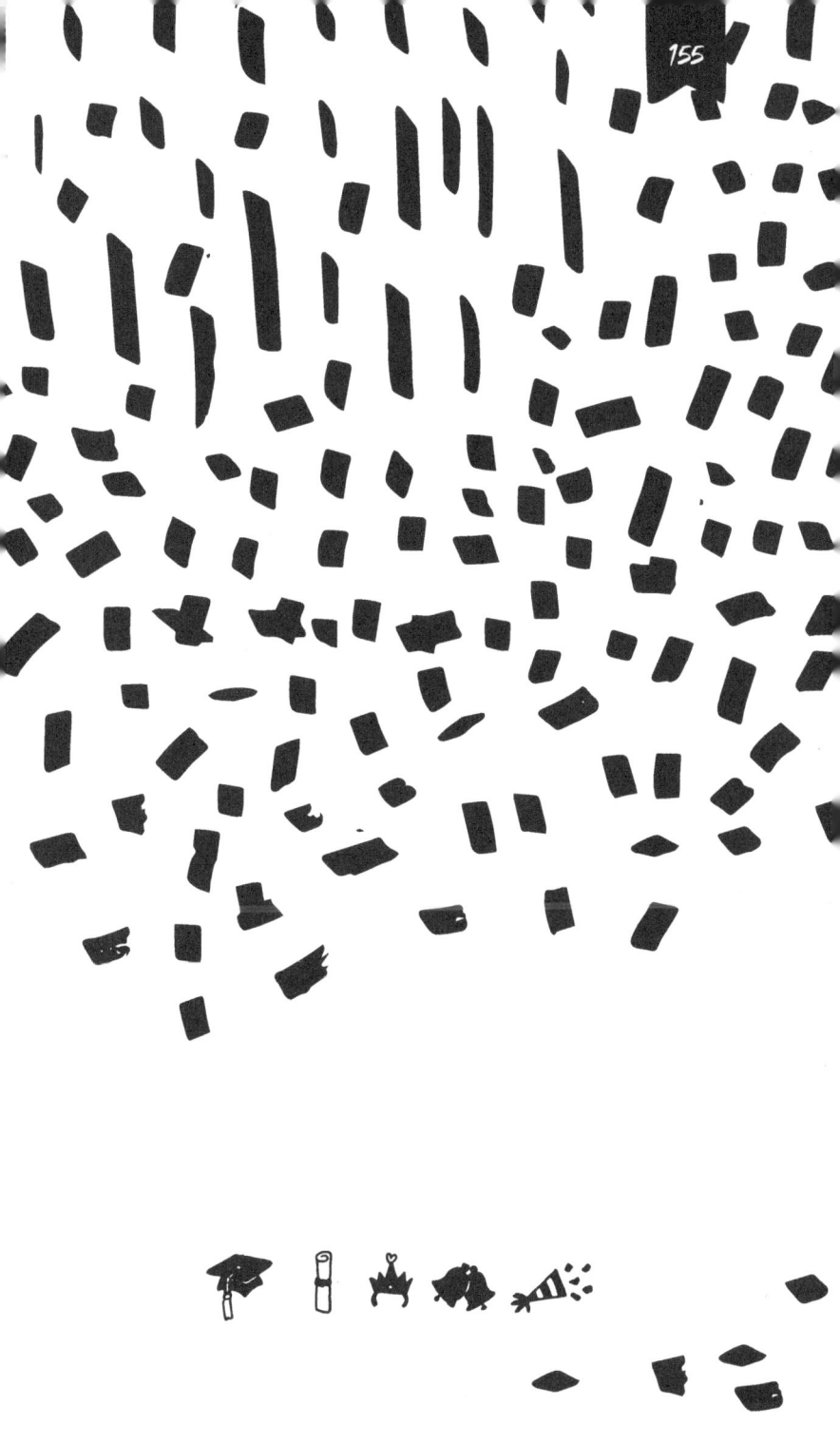

THE BIG DAYS OF YOUR LITTLE LIFE

PROM.

YOU PROBABLY DON'T WANT TO THINK ABOUT HIGH SCHOOL IN GENERAL, BUT THE MEMORIES YOU HAVE ABOUT PROM ARE SOMETHING YOU CAN NEVER SHAKE AWAY. IT WAS THE NIGHT FOR YOU TO BE A STAR AND DRESS TO THE NINES, RENTING OUT CHEAP TUXES AND BUYING PROM DRESSES OFF THE CLEARANCE RACK. NOTHING LIKE ITCHY POLYESTER FABRIC TO CHAFE YOUR SKIN AS YOU BOOTY DANCED AWKWARDLY TO TOP 40 HITS, ALL VAGUELY "REMIXED" (RE: CENSORED) BY A DJ SO THAT THEY WERE SCHOOL-FRIENDLY.

IF YOU RENTED OUT A LIMO, IT TOOK TEN OF YOUR FRIENDS TO CHIP IN JUST TO GET IT, NOT INCLUDING INSURANCE (BECAUSE TEENAGERS ARE CAREFUL, RIGHT?). THE VENUE WAS PROBABLY YOUR HIGH SCHOOL GYM, OR IF YOUR SCHOOL REALLY TRIED, THE VENUE HALL AT A LOCAL HOTEL. BUT HEY, YOU DIDN'T NEED RITZ AND GLAMOUR TO HAVE A GOOD TIME—WHEN YOU'RE WITH FRIENDS AND YOUR HIGH SCHOOL SWEETHEART, TO HELL WITH LIVING LIKE THE RICH AND FAMOUS, JUST PARTY ON!

make the best of it kid

The big days of your little life

Ivy League wasn't exactly an option for you.

Unless you're a genius, your chances for getting into Harvard or Yale are slim, especially when you can't just pay your way in like the 1%. As some one-percenters pledged for prestigious fraternities and sororities, you were wrecking opponents with your mad beer pong skills. It was state college for you, buddy, and all the scholarships you could manage to get with way too many student loans taken out in your name.

Does that make your education inferior? That's highly debatable. Some of the greatest minds went to state colleges and George W. Bush went to Yale. So. You decide.

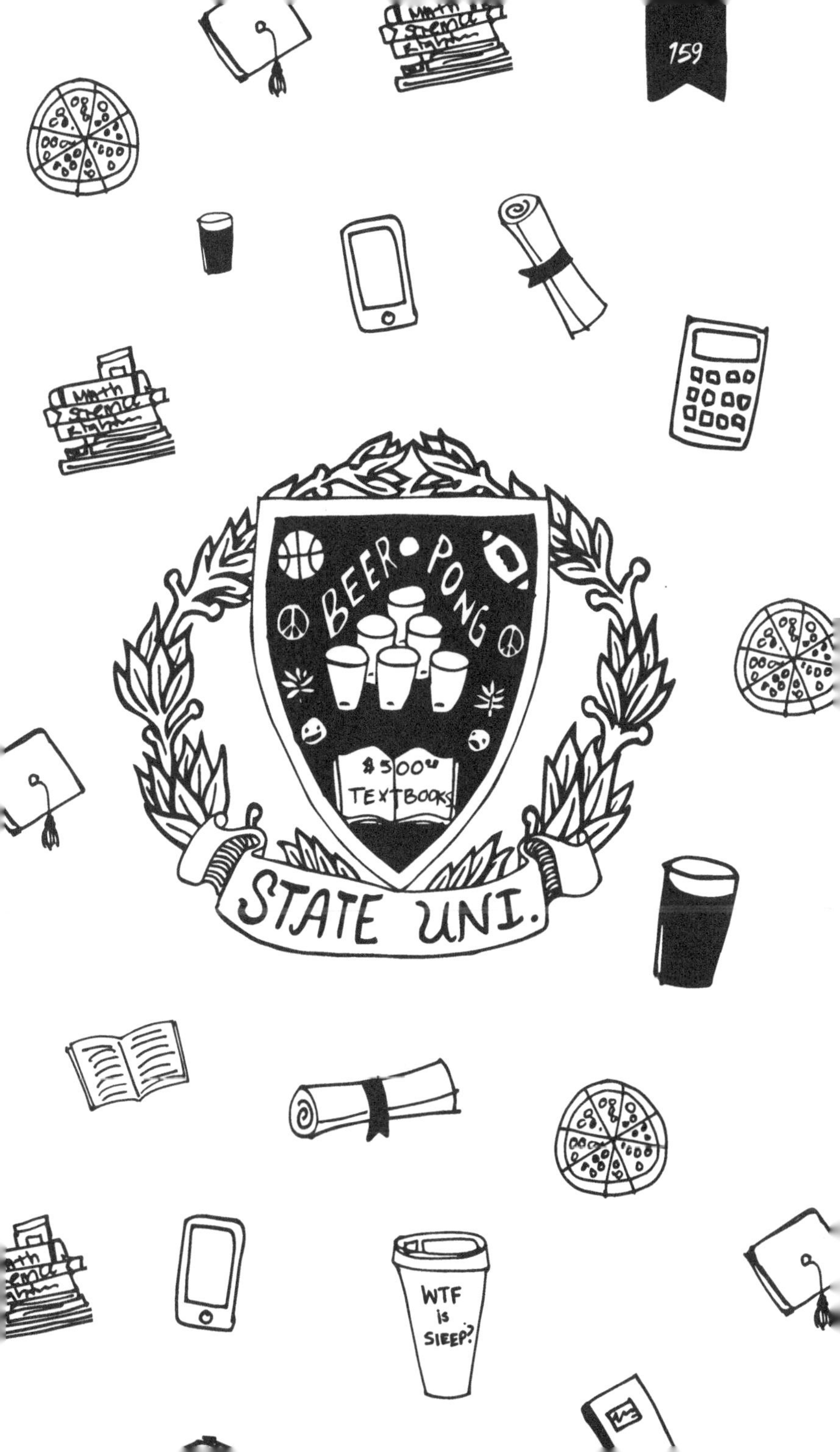
BEER PONG
$500 TEXTBOOKS
STATE UNI.
WTF is SLEEP?
Math

The big days of your little life

IF THERE'S NO OPEN BAR AT THE WEDDING YOU WERE INVITED TO, YOU REEVALUATE YOUR RELATIONSHIP WITH THE HONORED GUESTS.

Listen, you ask for one thing from your friends and that's: unlimited alcohol at the wedding. That's all. You'll pay for the evening clothes and fancy dinners, and you'll use up your vacation days just to go to this shindig and deal with people interrogating your life, but there better damn well be an open bar at the reception or so help you.

If you're expected to do the macarena after being asked why you don't have a marriage with kids yet, then you need a glass of whiskey. No questions asked.

Let's Celebrate

Wedding/Baby Shower Gifts: The Only Reason You Have Anything

If it weren't for wedding and baby showers, you'd still be cooking quesadillas on a hot plate. Whether you got a crockpot from your grandma or an entire china set from a friend, you are thankful for having friends who feel obligated to give you life's necessities as gifts.

And for the baby? You'll admit, you were kind of banking on that baby shower to provide everything you needed for raising the little one. Not because you're cheap and won't shower your own child with gifts, but because any money you do have is going straight to diapers. Your baby can be naked for all you care. As long as the little nugget isn't pooping all over the walls, you're as dandy as a peach.

The big days of your little life

YOU FORCE FUNDRAISERS ONTO YOUR COWORKERS, NOT INVITE THEM TO PARTIES.

When you ask for money for your child's fundraiser, it is just short of flat-out begging them. The only good fundraisers are the kind that offer cookies or chocolate, but sometimes you have to try to pawn off elaborate Christmas candles that suffocate you with cinnamon. But this is part of the job description and everyone knows it. You sell and you buy. It's for the children.

As for charity events, do you really want to go? You'd have to pay hundreds of dollars just for a plate of shrimp. At least four bucks can get you a box of thin mints. So, who's the real winner?

SHOULD I BUY COOKIES FROM THESE GIRL SCOUTS?

IS IT FOR THEIR CAMPING TRIP?

- YES →
- I DON'T KNOW? →
  - **DO YOU LIKE COOKIES?**
    - YES →
    - NOT REALLY →
      - **WHO ARE YOU**

YES, YOU HEARTLESS BASTARD

CONCLUSION OF SORTS

SO YOU'RE NOT RICH. WHO CARES?

MY FRIEND, YOU MAY NOT HAVE THE SUPERFICIAL LUXURIES THAT THE TOP 1% DO, BUT YOU STILL EXPERIENCE A HELL OF A LOT IN LIFE WITH MUCH MORE MEANINGFUL IMPACT. FOR EVERYTHING THE ONE-PERCENTERS HAVE, YOU JUST HAVE IT AT A SMALLER SCALE, BUT THE LOVE YOU SHARE WITH EVERYONE, THE STORIES YOU LAUGH ABOUT WHEN YOU LOOK BACK ON IT, AND THE MEMORIES YOU HAVE? THAT'S ALL YOU, BUDDY. NO ONE CAN TAKE THAT AWAY FROM YOU.

AND LOOK AT IT THIS WAY: WHEN YOU DO TREAT YOURSELF TO THE FINER THINGS IN LIFE, YOU KNOW YOU'RE APPRECIATING IT WAY MORE THAN SOME SPOILED BRAT OF THE WEALTHY CLASS.

LIFE TASTES SWEETER THAT WAY.

AUTHOR & ILLUSTRATOR BIO:

S.M. TORRES IS A SOUTH FLORIDIAN WRITER, WHO HAS DABBLED IN THE ART OF STAND-UP COMEDY AND FREQUENTLY TELLS JOKES QUIETLY TO HERSELF. SINCE GRADUATING EMERSON COLLEGE, SHE HAS PUBLISHED HER SHORT STORY FICTION IN THE ACENTOS REVIEW AND IS CURRENTLY TRYING TO FIGURE OUT HOW TO MAKE THE NEW YORK TIMES' BESTSELLER LIST AND ENTER THE 1% AT LAST.

CO-ILLUSTRATOR BIO:

ELINA DIAZ IS A WHIMSICAL ILLUSTRATOR, WHOSE ARTWORK CAN BE FOUND IN THE BROOKLYN ART LIBRARY AND THE UNIVERSITY OF MIAMI, AND WHICH HAS BEEN EXHIBITED IN TIMES SQUARE AND THE TURN BASED PRESS GALLERY IN MIAMI. SHE LIVES AND WORKS IN SOUTH FLORIDA, WHERE SHE DOODLES PRETTY THINGS FOR A LIVING AND IS THUS LIVING THE DREAM.